Paris

Nothing in Paris is what it seems, starting with its size:
it is a small city if you count only the nucleus of twenty
arrondissements with just over two million residents, but it is
Europe's second largest if you include the whole Île-de-France
region, which really you should. This separation of the centre
and the *banlieues* on its outskirts mirrors the even wider gulf
between the capital and the rest of the country, which has come
about through centuries of rigid centralism. The strength of
this gravitational force means that almost a third of the nation's
GDP and a quarter of its jobs are centred on the capital, but an
opposing force seems to push new arrivals away, both those from
France itself and from elsewhere, relegating them to the margins,
whether geographically and socially in a run-down *banlieue* or
more subtly for those who might live in the centre but are seen
by Parisians as foreign bodies, provincials. The glare of the City
of Light can be blinding, even for tourists: when faced with the
reality of a city so different from the cherished image portrayed in
films and books, some even develop a kind of culture shock known
as Paris Syndrome. But the shadows seem to be lengthening, too:
the Bataclan terrorist attacks, the protests of the *gilets jaunes*,
unrest in the *banlieues*, Notre-Dame in flames, record heatwaves,
unaffordable housing and the Coronavirus pandemic. This is
not just a series of unfortunate events, these are phenomena
– from overcrowding to climate change, from immigration to
the repercussions of globalisation and geopolitics – that all the
world's major cities must face. Despite these challenges, the
current mood in Paris remains one of renewal rather than defeat;
this we can see in a new approach to environmentalism and urban
planning – the dream of a city made up of numerous little centres,
ultimately all interconnected – a younger generation of chefs
fighting against the Michelin-star 'class system', the children of
immigrants protesting on the streets for the right to be accepted
as French and women casting off the stereotypes created for them
by the world of fashion. Is there anyone who genuinely believes
they can teach Parisians anything about staging a revolt?

Souvenir de Paris

Contents

The photographs in this issue were taken by the photojournalist and documentary photographer/video-maker **Cha Gonzalez**. She was born in Paris but spent her teenage years in Beirut, returning to the French capital to study photography and video-making at the École Nationale Supérieure des Arts Décoratifs. One strand of her work looks at techno parties as spaces where a stark yet tender vision of intimacy, beauty and people's ability to lose themselves is revealed through trance music and a strong interpersonal bond. Her works have been shown in various collective exhibitions, including *C'est Beyrouth* at the Institut des Cultures d'Islam in Paris in 2019 and *Nicéphore*, the Clermont-Ferrand biennial, in 2020. Her photographs were included in *Le Liban n'a pas d'âge*, a book marking the centenary of the state of Lebanon. She has worked for publications including *The Wall Street Journal*, *Elle*, *Libération*, *Le Monde* and *Causette*.

Paris in Numbers

INSTAGRAMMABILITY

The world's most Instagrammable cities

#hashtags (in millions)

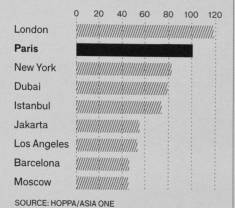

	0	20	40	60	80	100	120
London							
Paris							
New York							
Dubai							
Istanbul							
Jakarta							
Los Angeles							
Barcelona							
Moscow							

SOURCE: HOPPA/ASIA ONE

INEQUALITY

% of the population living below the poverty line (i.e. below €1,026/month or 60% of the median income) in the departments of Île-de-France

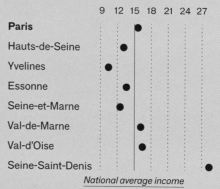

	9	12	15	18	21	24	27
Paris			●				
Hauts-de-Seine		●					
Yvelines	●						
Essonne		●					
Seine-et-Marne		●					
Val-de-Marne			●				
Val-d'Oise			●				
Seine-Saint-Denis							●

National average income

SOURCE: INSEE

MICHELIN STARS

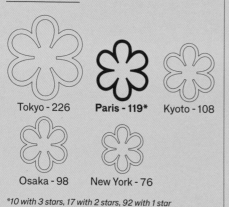

Tokyo - 226   **Paris - 119***   Kyoto - 108

Osaka - 98   New York - 76

*10 with 3 stars, 17 with 2 stars, 92 with 1 star

SOURCE: MICHELIN GUIDE 2020

CINEPHILES

Number of cinemas

Paris

312

Singapore

235

Shenzen

188

London

163

Chengdu

136

SOURCE: WORLD CITIES CULTURE REPORT

COMMUTING

Busiest railway stations in Europe

Passengers (millions per annum)

Paris Gare du Nord	**206**
Hamburg Hauptbahnhof	200
Paris Châtelet-Les Halles	**179**
Frankfurt Hauptbahnhof	164
Zurich Hauptbahnhof	154
Rome Termini	150
Munich Hauptbahnhof	127
Milan Centrale	120
Madrid Atocha	116
Berlin Hauptbahnhof	110
Paris Saint-Lazare	**107**

SOURCE: WIKIPEDIA

ÎLE-DE-FRANCE

The most populous regions in Europe

 1
Istanbul
15,067,724

2
Île-de-France
12,244,807

3
Lombardy
10,060,574

4
Greater London
8,982,256

5
Andalusia
8,427,405

SOURCE: EUROSTAT

LOUVRE

10.2M

visitors per annum, the highest number of any art gallery in the world (2018)

SOURCE: GUINNESS WORLD RECORDS

FLÂNEUR

2h15

Time to walk across the city from north (Porte de la Chapelle) to south (Porte d'Orléans)

FASHION FIGURES

€150

billion in direct sales

1M

jobs

2.7%

of total French GDP

SOURCE: FASHION KEY FIGURES (2016), IFM

WEALTH

EU regions with the highest GDP (2019)

Millions of euros

Upper Bavaria
274

Île-de-France
739

Rhône-Alpes
243

Madrid
240

Lombardy
399

SOURCE: EUROSTAT

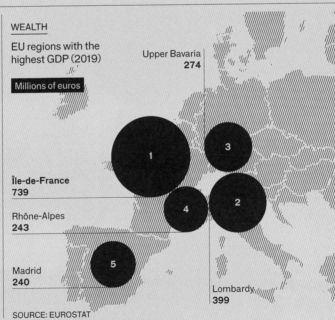

The Beaubourg Effects

THIBAUT DE RUYTER
Translated by Daniel Tunnard

Major architectural projects initiated by French presidents are scattered across Paris, but in recent times the fifty-year tradition of grand state interventions that began with the bold yet controversial Pompidou Centre has started to lose momentum. The baton has been taken up by private foundations linked to major luxury-goods brands, and artistic quality has suffered as a result. What follows is a love letter to the Beaubourg project but also a wry look at the entirely Parisian relationship between buildings and power.

The eastern façade of the Pompidou Centre.

What exactly is a city? Is it the sum of its buildings, whether historic monuments or everyday structures? Its population, how they eat and dress? The length and surfacing of its pavements, the presence of trees or street lamps, the billboards, the colours of its shutters, the style of its balconies? Or the neon signs in languages and alphabets that for some will be mysterious? (I recommend you check out Michel Gondry's beautiful video for Jean-François Coen's 'La Tour de Pise' to get a sense of the typographical richness of Parisian street signs.) Or, why not, the scent of its metro, a subtly different bouquet in every city, with hints of scorched rubber, hot oil and cleaning products? In short, when I talk about a city, I can approach it from any number of angles and express my love for it or – perhaps more likely – my hate. What's more, as Baudelaire wrote of the Paris of his day – and it still holds true – 'the shape of a city changes faster, alas, than the heart of a mortal'. Sometimes all it takes is a property operation with a well-planned strategy to kick-start the gentrification of a whole neighbourhood. A city is a complex organism, living and evolving, and Paris is no exception. Go away for a while, come back again and, like a friend you haven't seen for a long time, you recognise them immediately while noting the lines that have deepened on their face or their new hair-do. But the bouquet of a city's metro will probably be the same.

Whenever we find ourselves in a new town for the first time we often take the same approach to sightseeing, maybe by taking photos of monuments to show our friends – which also serves to prove that we've actually made the trip. As Susan Sontag wrote in her essay 'In Plato's Cave' (published in 1977 in the collection *On Photography*): 'Recently, photography has become almost as widely practiced an amusement as sex and dancing – which means that, like every mass art form, photography is not practiced by most people as an art. It is mainly a social rite, a defense against anxiety, and a tool of power.' In Paris, with the Sacré-Cœur, the Eiffel Tower, Notre-Dame (before, during or after the fire) and the Arc de Triomphe, there is plenty of scope when it comes to taking a selfie in front of a famous edifice with which everyone is familiar. But, unlike many other capitals – and this has been the case for some fifty years – the city has regularly endowed itself with buildings of great symbolic value known, unfortunately, as 'cultural facilities', signature architectures (or 'auteur' architectures, in the way one would describe the films of, say, Jean-Luc Godard) in recognisable forms that help redefine the territory while also marking a political era. These projects will often be decreed from on high, as one powerful person's desire to leave a mark on the city in the form of a building and help raise the value (both symbolic and economic) of some up-and-coming neighbourhood. This has become so common over recent decades that it is now a new French tradition, going by the appellation *grands projets présidentiels*.

THIBAUT DE RUYTER is a French-German architect, curator and art critic, who has lived and worked in Berlin since 2001. He has written for magazines such as *L'Architecture d'aujourd'hui*, *Artpress*, *Il giornale dell'architettura*, *Fucking Good Art*, *architectuul* and *Frieze d/e*. In addition to curating numerous international exhibitions – including *A Song for Europe* at the Victoria and Albert Museum, London, 2017 – he has edited a number of books on architecture, including *Stadt / bild* (Verbrecher Verlag, 2015).

Millions of visitors (2019)
Free admission, figures estimated

Notre-Dame (2018)	12.0*
Sacré-Cœur Basilica	11.0*
The Louvre	9.6
Eiffel Tower	6.2
Musée d'Orsay	3.6
Pompidou Centre	3.2
National Museum of Natural History	2.4
Cité des Sciences et de l'Industrie	2.4
Arc de Triomphe	1.6

SOURCE: PARIS TOURIST OFFICE

*

Obviously, the relationship between power and stone is nothing new. Kings and emperors built their palaces and castles, the Catholic Church its Gothic cathedrals and the French Republic its town halls, schools and ministries. (This is not to overlook the pyramids of Egypt or, in our own time, those structures commissioned by the likes of Apple, which erect iconic HQs that wouldn't look out of place in a sci-fi film but where the geometry – a perfect circle in the case of Apple – is just as minimal and radical as anything in ancient Egypt.) But let's get back to France and politics. It was in the mid-1970s that one president, a little more eccentric than his predecessors, decided to take on a cultural programme – a museum. Georges Pompidou was a statesman unlike his peers, and any number of things set him apart from the crowd, such as his independence and his love of the avant-garde. He smoked Marlboros (in homage to France's American liberators) but parked the cigarette in the corner of his mouth in the style of French agricultural workers, keen smokers of the legendary Gitanes Maïs. During one television interview at his country residence, he proudly showed the camera his pinball machine and demonstrated his skills. He loved avant-garde art and didn't care who knew it, even if it meant shocking the same bourgeois element that had swept him to power. So it was that when he moved into the Élysée Palace in 1969 he asked Pierre Paulin to provide the furniture, ordered works of modern art (Robert Delaunay, Jean Arp, Nicolas de Staël) and commissioned the artist Yaacov Agam to decorate one of the halls. Using op art in different tones of red, green, yellow and blue, Agam transformed the gold leaf and traditional decoration of this Parisian palace with up-to-date decor that wouldn't have looked out of place in a nightclub scene in a gangster flick. The walls were covered in multicoloured three-dimensional panels, the floor with a thick carpet and, in the centre of the room, there was a stunning polished metal sculpture that reflected the space and its colour scheme. This legendary hall is today on display at the Georges Pompidou Centre, a building that this president commissioned and which remains today the visible legacy of his mandate.

Above: Young people continue to meet in the piazza to the west
of the Pompidou Centre in spite of the ongoing renovation works.

THE PASSENGER   Thibaut de Ruyter

'Surprisingly, Parisians have given this place an Italian nickname, the "Piazza Beaubourg". I doubt this is in tribute to the nationality of Renzo Piano but rather a natural reaction to the feeling of openness and freedom that this space confers.'

It should come as no surprise then to learn that Pompidou had been thinking of founding a 'creation centre' since 1960, rejecting the backwards-looking terminology of 'museum' in favour of a multifunctional kind of place where dance, industrial and graphic design, architecture and cinema – but also a free-access public library – would come together in the heart of Paris. For the revolution of the Georges Pompidou Centre was not solely a matter of form, style and technology but a revolution of programme. As set out in the original competition, it was not at all a simple space where works of art could be hung on white walls. It might sound odd, but before it actually exists a building is a *programme*. Were I to launch a competition for the construction of social housing that's too cramped, I should not be surprised if the inhabitants feel less than happy to be living there. If I factor in draconian building regulations, I should not be surprised when the architects come up with somewhat banal solutions. In the case of the Georges Pompidou Centre, however, all such restrictions were thrown out. With an experimental programme, free rein for architects and a substantial budget, even before the first stone was laid the combination of these three factors made this building a very rare beast in the history of architecture.

Everything, absolutely everything, here is the stuff of legend. The competition was won in 1971 by two thirty-something unknowns, Renzo Piano and Richard Rogers. There were likely two main reasons for the jury's choice. First, it was chaired by Jean Prouvé, an architect who had for years defended the industrialisation of architecture and of building with metal; he would not have been unresponsive to their drafts. Second, a reason often cited was their choice of location. The land used for the construction of the Pompidou Centre is a square space called the Plateau Beaubourg. Rather than using the whole area available to them, Piano and Rogers sited their building on just half the land, creating a large pedestrianised square right in the middle of the city. (The important thing here is not so much the building as the space, the breath of fresh air that it brings to the urban environment.) To this day a quick survey of passers-by in Place Georges Pompidou reveals that feelings about the building are not unanimous. People tend to look at the structure itself, which they liken to a colourful factory, and do not realise the extent to which the architects created, above all, a 'piece of the city'. Surprisingly, Parisians have given this place an Italian nickname, the 'Piazza Beaubourg'. I doubt this is in tribute to the nationality of Renzo Piano but rather a natural reaction to the feeling of openness and freedom that this space confers. Aside from tastes and colours, the jury were keen on the idea of a new square in the city centre and could use it to justify their selection. One could write page after page on the inventiveness of the technical details, on the desire for flexibility of use, on the engineers' intelligence, on the radical separation between spaces for exhibition, services and distribution – but any good book on the history of architecture will tell you that.

If you were to ask a Parisian – or any French person who has visited the capital – there's a fair chance they'll have an anecdote about the Pompidou Centre, because the building is not simply an urban and architectural feat, it has become a part of the life of the city and of its inhabitants, just like the typography of its signs or the subtle odour of the Paris Métro. It could be a memory of hours spent flirting in the *piazza* or the presence of the man who comes almost every day to feed the pigeons on the corner of Rue Rambuteau and Rue Saint-Martin. Bearing bags of grain and who knows what else, he attracts the birds in such numbers that man and pigeons become one, an image that would not have displeased the surrealists.

My own anecdote dates back to the early 1990s. I was studying architecture in a provincial town but tried to spend as much time as I could in Paris, taking advantage of its cultural offerings, discovering and learning. Obviously, the Pompidou Centre was a must-see attraction, but you have to imagine a different building from the one you visit today. At the time of its conception the architects anticipated far fewer visitors; to give just one example of how this influenced their thinking, nearly all the exhibition spaces were fitted with carpets. It's a minor detail, but can you imagine a museum or any place welcoming visitors in the kinds of numbers that come to the Pompidou Centre with carpets? The greatest change, though, is that the numerous doors on to Rue Beaubourg used to be open, and whoever so wished could simply walk across the great hall without buying a ticket. The 9/11 New York attacks clearly brought about a revision of the security rules, and now, come rain or shine, visitors form a long queue as they wait to enter the building one at a time after passing through a metal detector. On this particular day my girlfriend and I entered via I don't know which side to go to the modern art section. One of the other visitors had quite a presence. Somewhat heavyset, with a large beard, barefoot on the carpet, he was carefully explaining the paintings to the young man next to him. The bearded man stood close to his companion, and, as he spoke, slipped his hand down his friend's trousers to fondle his buttocks, all the while waxing lyrical about the works of Pablo Picasso, Bernard Buffet and Francis Bacon. At a time when people didn't talk about same-sex marriage, this scene, amusing in itself, could have had the power to shock, but in this setting, in this context, in this building, it all seemed perfectly natural. Amused, I kept on walking. It was only when I turned around to get a better look at the gentleman's face that I realised it was Allen Ginsberg, and I smiled at this fortuitous encounter with one of my heroes. But I was very shy and didn't dare go up and speak to him.

*

I must now turn to a text of around five thousand words (that is, roughly the same length as the article you are reading now), written in 1977 by Jean Baudrillard: 'L'Effet Beaubourg' ('The Beaubourg Effect'). Once again, the Pompidou Centre can take pride in a rare thing, namely that a philosopher should dedicate a whole essay to it shortly after it opened. Baudrillard was more than critical. He attacked the architecture and the way the building operated for resembling a nuclear power station, an airport, a supermarket – in other words, places of flow management, whether of people, baggage, fluids, merchandise or energy. He saw it as an uncontrollable machine, offering 'cultural entertainment' for the masses, who were unaware but happy to participate in the catastrophe waiting to happen. And he even dreamed of the final disaster, of the steel structure of the Pompidou Centre collapsing under the weight of its far too numerous visitors ... You can agree or disagree with his architectural criticism, but you have to admit that he is talking about a reality that affects all contemporary museums. We now judge the success of an exhibition by the number of people it attracts, by the length of the queue at its entrance, by takings in the gift shop. Museums have become operations with quantified returns, just like nuclear power stations, airports and supermarkets. Such is the Beaubourg Effect, and it is the reality for so many cultural institutions. The building was significantly transformed by Renzo Piano between 1997 and 2000 to improve public access: the large pit that had occupied the ground floor was partly filled and a vast information desk installed in the middle of the entrance space. Although its appearance hasn't really changed much, it is no longer the somewhat whimsical and eccentric building of the 1970s criticised by Baudrillard and patronised by Ginsberg. It is a perfect flow-management machine, but one with outdated poetics.

Unlike all the other Parisian buildings willed into existence by politicians, the Pompidou Centre does not seek consensus. It is witness to an era when the media and opinion polls had less influence and when politicians were not afraid to fly in the face of public taste. (It is said that when

Pompidou saw the results of the competition he said to his staff, 'It's going to make people scream.') It dates from before the postmodern revolution that would serve as an excuse for false regionalism, the advent of banality, the lack of courage and a general populist formalism. (Some rare architects do still come up with interesting ideas – Aldo Rossi, Oswald Mathias Ungers, John Hejduk – but unfortunately they have never worked in Paris.) The Pompidou Centre is the utopia of the 1970s in building form, a mix of pop art, technology, functions and fictions, very much inspired by Cedric Price's Fun Palace project of the early 1960s.

*

But can a city be distilled to its cultural buildings alone? They are clearly our new temples and churches, places where we meet up as a family for social and intellectual experiences. The Beaubourg Effect later gave way to the Bilbao Effect. In 1997 the Guggenheim opened a new museum in a declining Spanish city. Unemployment was rocketing, industry was dying, people were leaving. The museum's arrival radically transformed the city, and tourists began to flood in, hotels and restaurants opened and what had been a run-down industrial port became a jewel in the crown of the tourism industry. One building was enough to transform an entire city, and this example paved the way for several others to seek their own Bilbao Effect (in France, one might think of the Louvre's gallery in Lens or the Pompidou Centre in Metz), but that was more than twenty years ago, and Paris isn't Bilbao. The city is now counting on the 2024 Summer Olympic Games, but this time what is at stake is linking, associating and connecting inner Paris (that is, within the Boulevard Périphérique ring road) and the suburbs in order to better manage flows in this mega-city of more than twelve million inhabitants. The future of Paris no longer lies in one building – in fact, it no longer lies in Paris. The upcoming Olympics has triggered an urban-development strategy of Métro lines and stations (a new network called Grand Paris Express), housing and facilities that should help to unify a highly fractured and socially divided territory.

People often forget that Paris was one of the centres of the Beat Generation, at a time when competition raged between Paris and New York to see which of the two cities should be the world's capital of the arts. One need walk only fifteen minutes from the Pompidou Centre and across the Seine to get to 9 Rue Gît-le-Cœur and stand before what was once the Beat Hotel. Allen Ginsberg and Peter Orlovsky moved there in 1957 and were joined by William Burroughs, who pitched up from Tangier to finish his celebrated novel *Naked Lunch* in 1959. While at the hotel Burroughs met Brion Gysin and Ginsberg wrote one of his most famous poems, 'Kaddish'. There is no trace left of any of that, however. The hotel is now Le Relais du Vieux Paris, and it charges upwards of €200 ($235) a night to stay in a room with a faux historic, somewhat kitsch decor. (Back in the day, the American writers shared a single bathroom with the whole establishment and had to wait, if they were lucky, a month between changes of bedding.) The city is cleaner than ever, and the name of the hotel – the Inn of Old Paris in English – recalls the verses of Charles Baudelaire, which seems appropriate.

Whether it is Rue Gît-le-Cœur (the Beat Generation), Rue Campagne-Première (Yves Klein, but also Eugène Atget, Nicolas de Staël, Man Ray, Arthur Rimbaud and a host of others), Rue de Verneuil (Serge Gainsbourg, Juliette Gréco, Michel Piccoli)

PARIS 2024

In the summer of 2024, all being well, Paris will become the second city after London to host the Summer Olympics three times, following the 1900 and 1924 games. After losing out in 2008 and 2012, the French capital won the bid after three other candidates withdrew, leaving Paris and Los Angeles to divvy up 2024 and 2028 between them. A strong point in Paris's favour was the ability to host 95 per cent of the events in pre-existing or temporary structures, making it possible to keep the budget to €6.8 billion ($8 billion), substantially lower than London or Tokyo. The Eiffel Tower will form the backdrop for the beach volleyball tournament as well as the open water and triathlon events on the Seine. Horses and riders will hardly be roughing it either at the Palace of Versailles, while skaters will compete in the garden of the Tuileries. Road cycling events will feature the classic arrival on the Champs-Élysées and some of the courts at Roland Garros tennis stadium will be converted for boxing and handball events. The biggest outlays will be the Olympic village and the swimming pool, both purpose-built close to the Stade de France. The football stadium is a semi-white elephant built for the 1998 World Cup, which only ever partly fulfilled its mission to regenerate the surrounding *banlieue*. The Olympics will offer a second chance, this time accompanied by a major transport project, the Grand Paris Express. One of the promises is that 85 per cent of all athletes will be accommodated less than half an hour from their competition venues – even though delays are already mounting.

Above: Lifts on the east face
of the Pompidou Centre.

Above: A photograph of the Pompidou Centre under construction.
Below: A view of the François Mitterrand Library.

or Rue Saint-Benoît (Marguerite Duras), there is many a Parisian street that has built a legend around a public figure who once lived there. True Parisians will tell you with pride that such and such a famous person lived 'just on that corner'. It may be this that politicians seek to tap with their grand projects, creating a mythology around their name by associating it with a building that tourists can photograph while poets, artists and composers have to make do with a simple plaque on an ordinary building.

While the Pompidou Centre was the first, every subsequent French president has followed suit, with varying degrees of success. Valéry Giscard d'Estaing initiated the competition for the Musée d'Orsay (ACT Architecture and Gae Aulenti, 1979–86), but he was no longer in office when it was opened by François Mitterrand in 1986. Mitterrand himself left the Élysée Palace in 1995 with the Louvre Pyramid behind him (Ieoh Ming Pei, 1983–9), the Cité de la Musique (Christian de Portzamparc, 1984–90), the Opéra Bastille (Carlos Ott, 1983–9), the Arab World Institute (Jean Nouvel, 1981–7) and the Très Grande Bibliothèque, the name given to the national library (Dominique Perrault, 1989–96) – and that's only the cultural programmes! Jacques Chirac left to the city of Paris the Musée du Quai Branly, which now bears his name, while Nicolas Sarkozy, after realising that he had greatly underestimated the importance of culture during his five years in power, extended the Palais de Tokyo a few weeks before the elections, a rush job that didn't include any real building work; the work that was undertaken can be summed up as the addition of a door that allowed public access to spaces not previously used. Finally, François Hollande opened the Philharmonie in 2015 – a project in which he did not really

have much interest but which, located on the Boulevard Périphérique, symbolises that the future of Paris is no longer simply *in* Paris but *with* its suburbs. Since taking office in 2017 Emmanuel Macron has yet to launch a project for a building that will one day bear his name – after all, you can't demand budget cuts, launch an austerity programme *and* have the money to build a new monument to yourself. Also, his current concern is more around town planning and the establishment of Grand Paris – a sensible urban plan, finally, to remove the divide between the city and its vast suburban sprawl. All the same, in 2020, after a year-long debate and having kicked around a number of ideas, the French state announced its decision to rebuild the roof and spire of Notre-Dame in an identical manner to what had been there before it burned down in 2019 (at least, its exterior; the original frame probably cannot be replicated). This will be the biggest architectural decision of Emmanuel Macron's presidency. Dresden, Potsdam and Berlin rebuilt their churches and castles after they were bombed during the Second World War in a style that connected historical imitation and contemporary technical needs. Politicians no longer dare to innovate, making the words *timidity* and *mediocrity* synonymous with *demagoguery* and *success*. And so it is in Paris today: 2021 is definitely *not* 1971.

*

In Paris buildings change names as easily as its streets and avenues, and presidents clearly reserve the most prestigious addresses for themselves. The city thus boasts a François Mitterrand Library, a Jacques Chirac Museum, a Georges Pompidou Centre. (In contrast, there is no Helmut Kohl Museum in Germany, no Willy Brandt Concert Hall – although

'In Paris buildings change names as easily as its streets and avenues, and presidents clearly reserve the most prestigious addresses for themselves.'

there is a library dedicated to the Brothers Grimm in Berlin Mitte.) This clearly arises from the centralisation of the French state – with the country still locked in an unhealthy Paris–provinces schism – along with the office of a directly elected president whose power and functions appear not so far removed from those of a monarch. But why would one man (France still hasn't had a female president) wish to leave his mark in this way? In the case of Mitterrand, who has often been described as having embodied some of the ideals to be found in Machiavelli's *The Prince*, there was clearly a somewhat megalomaniacal desire to remain in people's memories, even after his death. In other cases, it was more a matter of securing a few more votes in the elections. But Hitler and Mussolini also loved to build monuments, and Central Asian dictators happily continue this tradition. France is a democracy, and its presidents should be the equals of their fellow citizens.

I ought to mention here the Cité des Sciences et de l'Industrie, the Opéra Bastille, the Cité de la Musique, but unfortunately all these are worthless architecturally: the label *grands projets présidentiels* does not guarantee architectural quality. But one thing's for sure, the person who comes out top in this story is the architect Jean Nouvel. In the 1980s he built the Arab World Institute; in the 1990s it was the Cartier Foundation; in the 2000s the Musée du Quai Branly; and, finally, in the 2010s the Philharmonie. He worked under Mitterrand, Chirac, Sarkozy *and*

Hollande. Far be it from me to label him a political opportunist as, ultimately, all his buildings in Paris show intelligence in their context and form – and with the Arab World Institute he, too, just like Piano and Rogers, designed a pretty square so you can admire the façade of the building. In an age of façadism, in the Cartier Foundation he created a transparent, conceptual example of this castrating dogma, and while the Musée du Quai Branly and the Philharmonie are both rather louder buildings than their predecessors, they are examples of contemporary architecture in a city that has, for a number of decades, defined itself by assiduously guarding its heritage.

Today it is private foundations that indulge themselves: it started with the sublime Cartier Foundation (1994) by Jean Nouvel (yes, him), more recently Louis Vuitton by Frank Gehry and Lafayette Anticipations by Rem Koolhaas and the Office for Metropolitan Architecture. The post-war glory years of the Pompidou era, when presidents were prepared to go against public opinion and good taste, are very much in the past for politicians, but it is interesting to note how corporate foundations have taken hold of the baton. Real architectural, economic and cultural power lies elsewhere, and it is no longer the avant-garde that comes out on top. Mega-collections are the reflection of the art market at its apex, machines of public domination by and for money. At every opening a politician rejoices, thanks the public, poses for the cameras, trying to

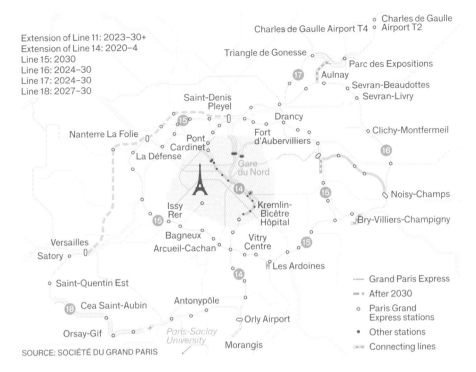

Extension of Line 11: 2023–30+
Extension of Line 14: 2020–4
Line 15: 2030
Line 16: 2024–30
Line 17: 2024–30
Line 18: 2027–30

Charles de Gaulle Airport T4 ○ Charles de Gaulle Airport T2

Triangle de Gonesse ○

Parc des Expositions

⑰ Aulnay ○

Sevran-Beaudottes
Sevran-Livry

Saint-Denis Pleyel ○

Drancy

Clichy-Montfermeil

Nanterre La Folie

Pont Cardinet
La Défense

Fort d'Aubervilliers

⑯

Gare du Nord

⑭

⑮ Noisy-Champs

Issy Rer
⑮

Kremlin-Bicêtre Hôpital

Bry-Villiers-Champigny

Versailles
Satory ○

Bagneux
Arcueil-Cachan

Vitry Centre

⑮

⑭

Les Ardoines

—— Grand Paris Express
– ▪ After 2030
○ Paris Grand Express stations
● Other stations
⋈⋈ Connecting lines

Saint-Quentin Est ○

⑱ Cea Saint-Aubin

Antonypôle

Orly Airport

Orsay-Gif ○

Paris-Saclay University

Morangis

SOURCE: SOCIÉTÉ DU GRAND PARIS

GRAND DESIGNS

Four new Métro lines and the extension of two existing ones; sixty-eight more suburban stations, each with land close by for new housing. Economic clusters around the city, chief among them the scientific and technological hub of Paris-Saclay to the south of Versailles, linked not just to the centre and the airports but also to each other. A new institutional structure bringing together the city of Paris and the 130 adjoining municipalities. This is the ambitious Grand Paris project, first championed by President Sarkozy in 2008 – although the idea dates back at least as far as Mitterrand's presidency – and progressed, with alterations and the removal of some elements of the original plan, by successive governments. It is western Europe's largest infrastructure plan, and it aims to transform the city into a major 21st-century metropolis, improving the quality of life of its inhabitants, correcting geographical disparities and building a sustainable city. The first and most explicit objective is to reduce the historic segregation between the 2.2 million residents of the centre, walled in and protected by the notorious and congested Boulevard Périphérique, and the ten million inhabitants of the outlying districts: the Grand Paris Express rail network will link the suburbs to each other, creating multiple centres, and promises to address the dual issues of prohibitive rents inside the city limits and hours of traffic jams outside. Such an ambitious programme inevitably attracts criticism, ranging from the high costs (which have already doubled between the initial plans and their 2018 revision) to the dominant role played by the private sector in delivering housing. The first stretches of the new Métro lines – automated and driverless – are due to open in 2024, and the whole project should be completed by 2030. Paris is preparing for the future by letting go of the idea that has always defined it: the conviction that it is the centre of the world.

One day after the fire that raged at Notre-Dame on 15 April 2019, President Macron announced that the cathedral would be rebuilt 'more beautiful than before'. The debate that followed focused on what is always a delicate issue, in Paris and elsewhere: restore or innovate? Macron was clearly in the innovators' camp, announcing an international competition for a plan combining 'tradition and modernity'. But it soon became clear that majority public opinion, backed, predictably, by the government's right-wing opposition, would prefer a more conservative solution. It was probably the threat of resignation from the chief architect for the works, Philippe Villeneuve – who is responsible for the maintenance of France's historic monuments – that convinced Macron to take a step back. The irony is, of course, that there was very little 'original' left of the cathedral that welcomed around twelve million tourists in the year before the fire: the most recognisable architectural and decorative features – from the gargoyles to the *flèche*, the neo-Gothic spire – were the work of Eugène Viollet-le-Duc, the brilliant and controversial architect in charge of Notre-Dame's 19th-century restoration. The current plan also includes a complete renovation of the parvis, the square in front of the façade, which comes under the jurisdiction of the city authorities. This might provide Macron with the opportunity for the contemporary 'architectural gesture' he would have liked for the spire, following the example of the Louvre Pyramid.

recover a little media glory. Still, Gehry does what Gehry does, and the OMA building has nothing spectacular about it (the firm recycled a beautiful idea from the 1990s that had originally been conceived for a house in Bordeaux). They don't make the city, they make image-buildings for a brand. They participate in *le marketing* and *le branding*, awful terms but which must here replace *patronage* and *generosity*, as they are far from disinterested. It is amusing therefore to note that Louis Vuitton turned to Frank Gehry. There is nothing particularly original in this, as it was through Gehry's work that the Bilbao Effect was born, and he signs off on prestigious cultural programmes all over the world. But Piano and Rogers weren't yet forty when they came up with the design for the Beaubourg, Jean Nouvel was thirty-five when he won the competition for the Arab World Institute, while the Fondation Louis Vuitton is the work of an 85-year-old. This same architect designed the American Center in 1993, in the Paris-Bercy area, which for some years was the cultural hub of the USA in France and was bought by the Cinémathèque Française – granted, it is a pretty building and well worth visiting. At the time Gehry still hadn't totally honed all his tricks and stunts, his recipes, and his architecture hadn't yet become the simple play of forms that it is today.

*

I regret not asking Allen Ginsberg what he thought of the Pompidou Centre, but I like to think that he saw it in much the same way that I did, as a unique, magical place, albeit one now historic and sick with its own success. The building, with its factory metaphor (Parisians often nickname it 'the Oil Refinery'), clearly marks the arrival of a new world, that of the cultural industry with its Hollywood films and phenomenal

Above: Tourists in front of Ieoh Ming Pei's Louvre Pyramids at the main entrance to the museum.

Above: Two visitors take in the view
from the top of the Pompidou Centre.

THE PASSENGER   Thibaut de Ruyter

budgets but also the exhibitions for which the public queue for hours and jostle with one another in the crowded exhibition spaces. What Baudrillard called the Beaubourg Effect has become a widespread disease. Still, an avant-garde poet such as Ginsberg, a friend of Andy Warhol and Jonas Mekas, having lived for a while on the other side of the Seine on Rue Gît-le-Cœur, must have liked this building. A place where you could walk barefoot on the carpet while slipping your hand down your friend's trousers as you admire a Francis Bacon canvas. The Pompidou Centre (like everything in Paris) has been sick ever since. Sick of being over-visited, sick of having to justify its existence and quantify its success through visitor numbers, sick of security measures imposed on a world living under the threat of terrorism. Different works have transformed the architecture, making it less flexible, less playful and more capable of managing the tide of visitors. The carpet has gone and, with it, the comfort of the visit. There remains an image, an icon of architecture and a man who comes to feed the pigeons at the corner of the broad, pedestrianised square.

I must now finish this tour with a somewhat secret spot that I have cherished for quite some time: the Mémorial des Martyrs de la Déportation, built by Georges-Henri Pingusson. It is located around half a kilometre from the Georges Pompidou Centre as the crow flies and a few metres from the Arab World Institute, and yet you will not have to elbow your way past tourists to get in. And it is not there to honour the memory of a single man (even though Charles de Gaulle personally took charge of its opening in 1962) but the several hundred thousand deported to concentration camps under the Vichy government during the Second World War. In the early 1950s Pingusson was contracted along with three others to construct a memorial, on the eastern tip of the Île de la Cité, directly behind Notre-Dame. Clearly it would be a challenge for any architect tasked with building in this place: how could you ever compete with the cathedral? Pingusson hit upon a brilliant and dramatic solution. Brilliant because, instructed to keep it as discreet and as low as possible, he buried his memorial completely and left a large open area at ground level that became the Square de l'Île-de-France, just as the Beaubourg project features an urban plaza; dramatic because, being below ground, to 'enter' the memorial you have to descend the stairs in two rough 'fault lines' in the concrete structure. While the monument is one of immaculate whiteness, it is rather like a descent into hell. You find yourself in a small triangular courtyard then enter some spaces that are just like a modern crypt. It's beautiful, elegant, stunning – above all, it's discreet. And therein lies perhaps the Pompidou Centre's one defect: this exuberant building, a symbol of the future and of innovation, has never sought to hide itself away. And all those that have followed – whether the Musée du Quai Branly, the Très Grande Bibliothèque or the Fondation Louis Vuitton – are loud and demand attention. Perhaps this is the real Beaubourg Effect: buildings flaunt their wares in the expectation of being photographed by tourists looking to be entertained. ➤

The Avenue of Revolt

LUDIVINE BANTIGNY
Translated by Simon Pare

BANQUE *olfea*

BANQUE POPULARE

A smoke grenade is set off in a crowd
of demonstrators in Paris.

In November 2018 thousands of people gathered in Paris to demonstrate against the hike in fuel prices and the high cost of living. Wearing hi-vis yellow vests, *gilets jaunes*, and chanting slogans inspired by the French Revolution and by the civil unrest of May 1968, they descended on the Champs-Élysées, 'the world's most beautiful avenue', a symbol of the power of the Republic and the inequalities in French society. For months they wreaked havoc. It was the only way to get their voices heard.

27

'We've never seen anything like it.' Stunned police officers say these words over and over again, according to an article in *Le Monde* on 16 March 2019. There is indeed something stupefying about a popular revolt targeting the Champs-Élysées, that monumental avenue and national symbol. Unexpected, unprecedented, unheard-of: the *gilet jaunes*, or 'yellow vests', movement is a truly spectacular thing. Even as it unfolds it feels as if nothing will ever be the same again. The combination of originality, suddenness, determination and intensity lends it a historic force. There are all kinds of odd scenes: barricades are set alight; protesters dressed as Marianne, the emblem of the French Republic, face off the police; some demonstrators commandeer a crane, while others drag armchairs out of a restaurant and sit on them in the middle of the road; shop windows are smashed ...

The target is the government and its inner sanctum, the presidential palace. A few months earlier, the occupant of the Élysée Palace came out with one of those phrases that at first sounds inconsequential: 'Let them come and get me!' The *gilets jaunes* took him at his word, and now fear is gripping the highest echelons of the state. The Champs is transformed into a battlefield. Footage of these confrontations is, by turns, bizarre and fascinating; 'magical' for some, terrifying for others. And word starts to spread that the protests are no longer stage-managed marches; they now have the symbols of power in their sights.

This sends tremors through a place that is both foreign and familiar: a picture-postcard avenue where the people have no rights but have come to claim them. This is the paradox of the Champs-Élysées: it is a highly political place, but it is somewhere that politics traditionally takes a back seat to tourism and shopping. Luxury goods exhibit their inaccessibility. Yet all of a sudden the Champs is repoliticised, showing itself for what it really is. It is in the nature of an uprising to shine a new light on places, to metamorphose them and alter their meaning. Occupying roundabouts transforms soulless places into communal places. Rebellion makes visible those who are invisible and whom the media have forgotten. Seizing the Champs exposes all the violence that underpins the supposed peacefulness of the social order,

LUDIVINE BANTIGNY is a professor at the University of Rouen who specialises in the history of social movements and political struggle, in particular the civil unrest in France in May 1968. Among her numerous publications are *1968: De grands soirs en petits matins* (Seuil, 2018), *La France à l'heure du monde: De 1981 à nos jours* (Seuil, 2013) and *Révolution* (Anamosa, 2019). Her latest book, *«La plus belle avenue du monde»: Une histoire sociale et politique des Champs-Élysées* (La Découverte, 2020), from which this article is extracted, is a political and social history of the Champs-Élysées.

'The area is unrecognisable: a lorry blazes in the middle of the road, a bank is in flames, swirling smoke gives the street scenes an apocalyptic feel, and the whole area is cordoned off.'

and for the protagonists it is also a chance to be seen, listened to – and perhaps even heard. That is the strength of a riot in all its violence and joy. A riot in which the excitement of being in this unlikely place is tinged with shock. 'We're here,' the *gilets jaunes*' chant goes – somewhere no one would ever have expected them to be.

'TIME FOR OUTRAGE!'

Act 1. On 17 November 2018 tens of thousands of *gilets jaunes* take over roundabouts, block toll booths and occupy roads and motorways. Others decide to go to the Champs-Élysées to protest. By noon a thousand people are converging on Place de l'Étoile, the intersection that has the Arc de Triomphe at its centre. The plan at first is to block the traffic by marching over the pedestrian crossings. Soon, however, the crowd invades the avenue. Waving French flags and singing the 'Marseillaise' at the tops of their voices, the protesters encourage the riot police to join them. But the police respond with grenades, and so it becomes a matter of evading them, dodging them, giving them the slip. Very quickly the protest morphs into a different kind of demonstration. It is made up of people of all ages. Their slogans and yellow vests talk of taxes, buying power and a state they don't respect and that doesn't respect them. '*Macron démission*' ('Macron resign') is the phrase binding the movement together. 'Wake up, it's time for outrage!' one placard reads. Barricades are erected to the thrumming of motorbike engines. The scenic avenue has become a field of battle.

A week passes, and the *gilets jaunes* are back on the Champs. The Twitter account of the mayor of Paris, Anne Hidalgo, seems oblivious to the situation, suggesting that people 'come and admire the fantastic Christmas lights on the Champs-Élysées'. Botched communications, her adviser Matthieu Lamarre quickly acknowledges. Everything is subverted and put to a different use, including a line from the Joe Dassin song 'Les Champs-Élysées', which goes, '*Je m'baladais sur l'avenue, le cœur ouvert à l'inconnu ...*' ('I was walking down the avenue, my heart open to all things new ...') which is reworked as '*J'manifestais sur l'avenue, mais mon gilet leur a pas plu ...*' ('I was protesting on the avenue, but my vest caused a real to-do ...'). The protesters get very close to the Élysée Palace, to within a hundred metres or so. The area is unrecognisable: a lorry blazes in the middle of the road, a bank is in flames, swirling smoke gives the street scenes an apocalyptic feel, and the whole area is cordoned off. These pictures are broadcast around the world. The Italian newspaper *La Repubblica* talks of guerrilla warfare. The next day a journalist from the BFM TV news channel reports live that the *gilets jaunes* have ripped up the cobblestones from a hundred-metre stretch of the avenue. Fact-checking confirms that this particular section was already under repair and the protesters are not to blame for the missing cobblestones. This misrepresentation

THE PARIS MASSACRE

One of the darkest episodes in the history of political demonstrations in Paris took place on 17 October 1961. That day a crowd of thirty thousand Algerians, who had been rallied by the Algerian-nationalist National Liberation Front (FLN), demonstrated against the racist curfew decreed by the prefect of police for Paris, Maurice Papon, which prohibited Muslims from circulating after 8.30 p.m. France was in the final throes of the bloody Algerian War, which lasted from 1954 to 1962 and was marked by guerrilla operations on both sides: between the end of August and the beginning of October 1961 alone the FLN had killed eleven policemen in Paris. Tension was in the air, and the demonstration turned into a bloodbath: according to some historians, on Papon's orders the police killed as many as three hundred people, although when President Hollande issued a long-overdue official apology half a century later, the figure admitted to was forty. They were not only beaten to death but also thrown into the Seine, some tied up in sacks while still alive. It was also many years before Papon was convicted – and not for this massacre, which still remains unpunished, but for his role in the deportation of Jews during the Vichy years. Having gained independence, Algeria also sullied its own reputation with a killing spree that claimed hundreds of victims in Oran in 1962, a settling of scores with the *pieds noirs*, the French, other Europeans and Jews who at the time formed a community of around a million people in Algeria. By the end of the 1960s only fifty thousand were left, most having returned to their 'homeland', even though for many this so-called return was their first visit, experiencing a similar fate to that of the *retornados* from the newly independent Portuguese colonies in the 1970s.

THE PASSENGER   Ludivine Bantigny

feeds the drama. Three days later, after a meeting with the ecological transition minister François de Rugy, Éric Drouet and Priscillia Ludosky (an entrepreneur who in May 2018 launched the petition 'For a reduction in retail fuel prices' and which now has well over a million signatures), whom the French media identified as the spokespeople of the *gilets jaunes*, call for a second demonstration on the Champs for the following Saturday. And every Saturday after that.

Act 3, on 1 December, shows the first signs of a huge movement coming together. It includes railway workers, anti-racist groups, students, young people from the working-class *banlieues* and people of many different political persuasions. The SUD rail union appeals for people to 'jump aboard the protest train', and the Comité Adama – a collective that campaigns for justice and truth in the case of Adama Traoré, who died on 19 July 2016 in police custody in Persan at the age of twenty-four – emphasise the need for solidarity: 'As people from working-class neighbour-hoods, we, too, generally do the most precarious jobs for miserable wages.' This appeal makes a link between the *banlieues* and isolated rural areas: 'We, too, some-times have to drive for hours to get to our workplaces in factories and warehouses as cleaners or security guards. Many of us are unemployed – 40 per cent in some places.' It concludes: 'Let's forge an alliance of equals.' The philosopher and economist Frédéric Lordon also invites citizens to 'pour all our anger into the cauldron'.

The police rapidly kettle the protesters around the Arc de Triomphe and keep them there for several hours. The monument is defaced with ironic and vengeful graffiti: 'The *gilets jaunes* will triumph'; there is a slogan borrowed from Chile – 'The people united will never be divided'; and – 'We're

right to rebel.' A group of protesters batter down the reinforced door with a concrete bench and a metal bollard and stream into the Arc. Someone damages a plaster statue, a copy of a sculpture by François Rude; it loses an eye. However, the protesters are determined to protect the flame of the unknown soldier and keep watch over it. Herein lies the ambiguity of the place and the moment: the *gilets jaunes* invading the Arc de Triomphe do not reject patriotic values, let alone the Republic. Ali, the first to enter, says later that he was enraged by suggestions that he was a fascist. The main objective, he says, was to plant the French tricolour at the top. The monument is now a strategic location. Barricades are erected where the avenues enter the roundabout, and there are extremely violent clashes. Caught off guard by the speed of events, the riot police make a show of force, launching ten thousand grenades and bringing in water cannon and even a helicopter, which hovers over the scene. 'We were reluctant to call it in because it makes it look as if the city's under siege,' a high-ranking officer remarks.

'The targets', the Paris police chief Michel Delpuech recognises, 'are property, smart cars, banks, upmarket areas of town. To the *gilets jaunes* Paris symbolises two things: power and wealth.' Some luxury cars do indeed end up as burned-out shells. The determined protesters force a company of riot police to retreat. A senior civil servant admits that this is now an insurrection.

On 8 December the Place de l'Étoile is again surrounded by gendarmes and armoured cars, which, since the war, have only been seen here during parades. Paris police headquarters instructs shops to lock their doors and shutter their windows. Jean-Noël Reinhardt, the president of the Comité des Champs-Élysées, calls the situation a disaster. Half of the avenue's shops don't open that day. There is no let-up in the protests.

On 15 December there is an impressive stand-off between five women dressed as Marianne, the personification of the Republic, and the riot police stationed on the Champs-Élysées. The women stand there, their bodies a political statement. Not far away protesters kneel on the cobblestones, symbolically recalling an incident in Mantes-la-Jolie, a working-class town fifty kilometres west of Paris, where three days earlier police forced dozens of teenagers, most of them Arab or black, to kneel with their hands on their heads like hostages. 'Finally, a well-behaved class,' was one policeman's comment that was widely reported after the event. This powerful act establishes a bond between two places – the Champs-Élysées and Mantes-la-Jolie – that could not be more different, nullifying the social distance between them in a surge of solidarity, as if this luxurious avenue, the most privileged place imaginable, has become an avenue of the people.

A week later a procession is hit by a hail of grenades. A group of protesters retaliate by attacking some police officers on motorbikes who quickly withdraw, but a member of the rearguard draws his gun and points it at the crowd. Fortunately a tragedy is avoided. On 29 December a protester in a Phrygian cap and a gold cape holds aloft the sword and scales of justice. 'Insurrection is the people's duty,' this allegorical woman shouts at the assembled police officers, echoing the words of the 1793 version of the Declaration of the Rights of Man and the Citizen: 'When the government violates the rights of the people, insurrection is for the people and for each portion of the people the most sacred of rights and the most indispensable of duties.' The present permeates the past and brings it alive on an avenue so often swept by the winds of history. The *gilets jaunes* are obsessed with revolutionary references, and so invading the Champs-Élysées equates to a second storming of the Bastille. Once again the aim is to capture the seat of power, its summit, a place where wealth and all the powers of social domination are concentrated, a symbol and a metaphor for yawning inequalities.

The violence alters the balance of power, but opinion among the *gilets jaunes* is divided. For some, the *casseurs* – extremist vandals – are repellent, while others regard violence as a necessary phase, as it has been in every other rebellion in history. The fact that the state is starting to back down goes to prove this, they say.

'Violence doesn't discredit the movement. It's necessary to shake things up,' says Laurent, an unemployed man in his fifties who has been protesting on the Champs-Élysées since the start of the uprising.

'The clashes do damage our image, but we won't get anywhere by doing nothing,' reckons Anthony, a thirty-something who has come all the way from the Gard department in southern France. 'We're pacifists, but if we can't make our voices heard something has to give. Things can't go on like this.'

'It isn't easy to make yourself heard,' says Françoise, a retired postwoman. 'We don't intend to be violent, but they force us to be.' She earns only €780 ($930) per month and has come to protest about rising living costs.

Right: A litter bin smoulders during a *gilets jaunes* demonstration.

> '**Aggressive police operations often drive people to violence. One learns by doing, and this goes for violence, too – by facing it, resorting to it, reacting to it.**'

Refrigeration specialist Gilles has travelled here from Caen in Normandy. He's here 'in solidarity' and says, 'I'm not asking for anything for myself. I don't mind paying taxes, I just want them to be put to good use.' He remembers May 1968, and the current protests remind him of those events. 'It's good that the youngsters are rebelling.'

Many people who went out on to the streets in 1968 had no intention of doing battle either but still ended up picking up cobblestones and hurling them. Aggressive police operations often drive people to this. One learns by doing, and this goes for violence, too – by facing it, resorting to it, reacting to it. This is how events are shaped: their protagonists act in a way they wouldn't have imagined two weeks, two days or even two hours beforehand.

It's no surprise that when calls for an Insurrectionist New Year's Eve are put out, anxious commentators are alarmed. Several thousand *gilets jaunes* are out on the Champs-Élysées on 31 December to ring in the new year with some satirical carols. (One example: 'Little Emmanuel [Macron]/ And all your loyal cabinet/You better run like hell/And leave us to celebrate'.) But this isn't a truce, and the *gilets jaunes* handing out flowers to the police does nothing to dial down the tension.

On 8 January 2019 the philosopher Luc Ferry, a former minister in the government of Nicolas Sarkozy, urges police officers to use their guns – and not just police officers. 'We have the fourth largest army in the world,' he says. 'It can put a stop to this bullshit.'

'They should call in the army and start shooting,' a shopkeeper says during an interview with the LCI television channel, echoing Ferry's comments.

Involve the army in the crackdown? The government is seriously considering it. Its spokesman, Benjamin Griveaux, entertains the possibility, but the heads of the armed forces don't share this position, and so the government is forced to backtrack.

HOLLOW LAUGHTER, OUTRIGHT FEAR
This suggestion of military intervention comes after Act 18 of the movement on 16 March 2019. Several shops on the Champs-Élysées are looted that day. Incendiary devices cause a number of blazes. A newsstand at number ninety-nine is gutted by flames. A bank burns briefly, and firefighters have to rescue a woman and her child from the second floor of the building.

And then Fouquet's is sacked. The front of the famous restaurant goes up in flames. However, the blaze doesn't appear to have been caused by protesters but by police tear-gas canisters landing on its awning. In any case, this incident has a startling impact, and commentators rush to express their outrage. Emmanuel Macron's assessment is that it is an assault on the Republic itself. In an editorial in the extreme-right-wing weekly *Valeurs actuelles*, on 12 April 2019, the journalist Jean-Marc Albert declares himself offended that 'the *casseurs* took full responsibility for their act. They thought it completely normal to set fire to an iconic place where the elite dines. This is to disregard the tumultuous history of restaurants, which were originally places where those in power were challenged,' his argument being that Voltaire and Rousseau used to meet at Le Procope, an 18th-century hub of subversive activity. According to Jean-Michel Aphatie, a radio and TV pundit, to suggest that the brasserie is a 'symbol of the oligarchy' is similar to a Taliban discourse, and he tweets that the *gilets jaunes* movement is 'both horrible and shocking'. Political journalist Christophe Barbier goes even further on BFM TV, declaring that it is not only Fouquet's that has been targeted but 'the entire system of capitalism, commerce and representative democracy; in a nutshell, everything the West stands for is being attacked by nihilists'.

One new development is that those on the side of the *gilets jaunes* approve the ransacking of the restaurant – or at least many refuse to 'condemn' it as they are being urged to. Fouquet's and its (rich) patrons don't inspire much sympathy. The following comments are proffered to outstretched microphones: 'This place represents money, and we don't have any money'; 'People are so fed up that they won't even listen'; 'It's a way of grabbing the attention of the elites who look down on us'; 'I'm almost glad it happened. I think maybe people will listen to us now'; 'No, I don't condemn it. Tough!' No hint of compassion for the avenue either, this symbol of brazen wealth. Many people emphasise other, less symbolic forms of violence. For them the real violence is social violence. 'Fouquet's is nothing. Just wait until the *gilets jaunes* destroy maternity clinics, close schools, dismantle the courts, gut the hospitals. Watch the outrage then!' 'The government are the real *casseurs*,' reads a banner unfurled on the Champs-Élysées. The media's sympathy for Fouquet's merely serves to highlight its

indifference to the plight of the men and women who never make the front pages: all the sacked workers, the hundreds of homeless dying on the streets, the unemployed, the people in precarious jobs, the undocumented migrants, the young people killed by the police …

There is a shift in strategy. Although many commentators draw a sharp distinction between black blocs and *gilets jaunes*, the latter are no longer so quick to distance themselves.

'Everyone used to be scared of the black blocs, but now people see them as an asset,' explains John, an organiser who has come from Nancy. 'They get things done. We're too peaceful.'

'Up to now I'd step in to stop any vandalism. Now I just think, "Oh well",' says Jennifer, a forklift-truck operator and mother of two. 'I saw them wrecking Fouquet's, the symbol of the oligarchy, and I can't say I agree with it, but I no longer disapprove.'

Ana, a postwoman, thinks the same. 'It's great because the bourgeoisie are so safe in their little bubble that to get them to give in they need to feel physically scared, scared for their own safety.'

'We've learned that we are heard only when things get broken,' says Johnny, the director of a day-care centre in the Ardennes. 'Macron has to accept he's toast.'

Johnny's use of a burning metaphor is probably accidental, but people do take a malicious pleasure in coming up with

Page 36: A car vandalised during a *gilets jaunes* demonstration (**top**); a mannequin in the window of a luxury boutique in Paris (**bottom**). **Page 37**: Police in riot gear on the Champs-Élysées.

'On 11 October the environmental group Extinction Rebellion occupies the avenue, proclaiming that "the only way to enter a better world is to break in".'

jokes about the burned-out Fouquet's: 'It's usually the bill that burns your fingers'; 'A nice chargrilled steak'; 'Do they still serve *crème brûlée*?' Thirsting for revenge, 'a horde of rich Parisians is on their way to destroy a Burger King in Pantin'.

Even the conservative daily *Le Figaro* notes the irony on 18 March: Fouquet's calls to mind Nicolas Fouquet, King Louis XIV's superintendent of finances, who was punished for flaunting his wealth. His motto was *Quo non ascendet?* (What heights will he not scale?), which the paper reworks as: '*Quo non descendet?* one wonders this morning at the sight of the devastated Fouquet's.'

A few days later a wall of sheet metal goes up around the restaurant. In his column in the left-wing *Libération* on 29 March, author Sylvain Prudhomme mocks its opulence: 'Oh, the consummate design, the top-notch machining. Such an exquisitely refined carapace, right down to the finish. Fouquet's is absolutely incorrigible – even their armour-plating is more bling-bling than anyone else's. This time, I'm afraid, they've given the world something perhaps only they were capable of: the very first platinum palisade.' Some people think it'll be a magnet for metal lovers ... What's undeniable is that the restaurant is 'armoured'.

Meanwhile, criminal proceedings commence. An auxiliary nurse named Ambre and a train driver called Franck find themselves first in custody and then in court for taking four forks and a stool, being accused of theft and receiving stolen goods. Both deny stealing anything. A video presented by their lawyer, Arié Alimi, clearly shows one of the restaurant's security guards picking up a jar of cutlery and some items from the floor and handing them out to people nearby. Eventually the magistrate's court dismisses the case on a technicality without further deliberation.

Some commentators do spare a thought for the staff at Fouquet's. The restaurant's management reassures everyone that everything possible will be done to ensure that 'colleagues' don't lose out. Staff will continue to receive their wages. Incidentally, in the hotel above the restaurant it's business as usual. What does prompt some bemusement, however, is that these same commentators have seldom shown much interest in the fate of workers whose factory has closed down. On 13 July the refurbished brasserie once more opens its doors. The front of the restaurant has been entirely redone, although the awning is now made of cotton rather than acrylic – because apparently cotton doesn't burn so easily. There is another announcement that same day: the Barrière group – which owns Fouquet's as well as a reported thirty-six casinos, eighteen hotels and more than 120 restaurants with a total estimated turnover of $1.42 billion – plans to open a Fouquet's in Abu Dhabi, the capital of the United Arab Emirates.

The police presence grows ever more threatening, but still the *gilets jaunes* return to the Champs, overcoming their fear and ready to break taboos. On 14 July, despite the security forces keeping the protesters at bay, Emmanuel Macron is whistled and booed during the Bastille Day parade. Anyone carrying a yellow balloon, not to mention wearing a yellow vest, is booed. The unlikeliest offences are punished as a hail of fines and charges rains down on the sunny Champs. When evening comes new barricades go up, and some are ablaze by nightfall. With each new act the question is: what's going to happen on the Champs-Élysées? There is a blanket ban on demonstrations, but the *gilets jaunes* keep on coming. On 21 September, during Act 45, they retake the Champs despite seven thousand police officers being deployed. Tourists find themselves caught up in the clouds of tear gas, too, and the pictures are replayed endlessly across the world.

A few weeks later, on 11 October, the environmental group Extinction Rebellion occupies the avenue, proclaiming that 'the only way to enter a better world is to break in'. Skill, agility and speed: the Arc de Triomphe is more heavily guarded than ever, but XR activists manage to drape their organisation's banner from the monument. The visual impact is clear and deliberate: the idea is to 'create an image' by analysing, manipulating and subverting the society of the spectacle. 'End of the world, end of the month, same culprits, same struggles' – once more the slogan rings out, but this time it's for a common cause.

WHAT DO THE PEOPLE WANT?
So what are these struggles about? First and foremost, they are against the high cost of living. In the current situation fuel prices have become a major issue. The 'carbon tax', a national tax hike on the consumption of energy commodities, certainly lit the touch paper, but popular revolts are not a reflex reaction to economic hardship – they are not merely 'rebellions of the belly' – they

THE 'BLING-BLING' BRASSERIE

Founded in 1899 by the drinks manufacturer Louis Fouquet (with a silent 't'), Fouquet's (with the 't's' pronounced in the English way) immediately became an institution on the Champs-Élysées. Early in its history it became a meeting place for aviators – the most glamorous heroes in the early 20th century – after Brazilian pilot Alberto Santos-Dumont, in 1903, 'parked' his airship at his house at number 114 and went to celebrate the feat over the road at Fouquet's. During the 1930s the clientele was dominated by people working in the film industry – it was where negotiations were conducted and contracts signed – and over the following decades it played host to a succession of the most famous names from the silver screen, from the *nouvelle vague* to Gérard Depardieu. In 1990, to save the institution from collapse, a committee of VIPs successfully had the brasserie registered as a historic monument. It was acquired in 1998 by the Barrière group, which operates casinos and hotels, and, almost inevitably, because of its history and its location, the restaurant became a symbol of the capital's elite. In 2007 the newly elected Nicolas Sarkozy chose to celebrate his presidential win at Fouquet's with a sumptuous dinner attended by a hundred top politicians, business leaders and celebrities. The party went down in the country's political history and set the tone for the presidency of the man subsequently nicknamed the 'bling-bling' president through his love of the good life and his circle of powerful friends. And, like Sarkozy, Fouquet's has never managed to shake off a reputation for hubris (not that it has tried very hard) that made it a target for the rage of the *gilets jaunes*.

vent an experience of contempt, a sense of injustice and their corollary, an aspiration to be acknowledged, respected and treated with dignity. The uprising of the *gilets jaunes* is just the latest example. It calls into question the very foundations of democracy and the distribution of wealth, and that it does so Saturday after Saturday on an avenue of such splendour and luxury – and power – lends it even greater force and meaning.

It is an intergenerational movement that includes as many young people as pensioners. According to a study published in 2019 in the prestigious *Revue française de science publique*, many of the latter 'have been through hard times, either personally or through having to provide regular financial assistance to their grown-up children'. Women and men are equally represented. The unemployment rate among the *gilets jaunes* is higher than in the general population, around 16 per cent compared with a national average of 10 per cent, according to a collective sociological survey. The *gilets jaunes* who took part in the aforementioned study describe their precarious circumstances: 25 per cent say they live in a household with a monthly income of less than €1,200 ($1,400), 50 per cent earn under €2,000 ($2,400) and 75 per cent under €2,900 ($3,450). The *gilets jaunes* are workers, employees (many of them temps), low-skilled, self-employed people and, to a lesser extent, intermediate professionals across a range of sectors – many public-sector workers and, in the private sector, lots of hauliers as well as auxiliary nurses, cleaners and hospital staff. It is a working-class revolt.

Pages 40–1: A demonstrator in front of the Arc de Triomphe.

A social scientist and, like many *gilets jaunes*, a temporary worker in a variety of different sectors, Tristan immediately identifies with the movement and goes to the Champs-Élysées with thousands of others 'to protest, or rather to exist, to exist in the eyes of the world'. He doesn't know much about the Champs. He lived in Burgundy for thirty years and has probably only been here once before, 'in a rush' on a school trip. The thoroughfare might be described as 'the most beautiful avenue in the world', but he is 'constantly haunted by a feeling that this beauty has been hijacked'. He has lived in Paris for three years now without ever coming here. Why would he? Certainly not for 'Fouquet's, the extravagant window displays, the overpriced drinks, the Arc de Triomphe, which is nothing but a reminder that victory is all about massacring people. Then, out of the blue, real beauty emerged. When all these people, most of them country folk like me, seized the Champs. There was this surge of collective power as we formed a human chain to dismantle some scaffolding and build a huge barricade with it. None of us knew anyone, but we were in it together – not to confront the police at all costs but to assert our dignity. That day, fed up with being regularly humiliated, ignored and ridiculed, we said "Enough", and we won. We won the right to our dignity.'

Marion, an artist, author and actress, defines herself as a 'class defector', a feminist and a *gilet jaune*. She describes how it felt to demonstrate in this 'smart neighbourhood' alongside working-class men and women like herself. 'For the first time in my life, as someone who's ashamed when I pass well-dressed people in the street, when I have to introduce my parents to my rich friends' parents, when my classmates used to bump into my uncles in the street, when I had to describe the house where

'"Fed up with being regularly humiliated, ignored and ridiculed, we said 'Enough', and we won. We won the right to our dignity."'

my grandparents lived ... for the first time I wasn't ashamed. I wasn't ashamed when we passed the line of rich, smartly dressed people in their fur coats queueing for the museum and they looked at us in shock and fear. I was proud. Proud to be marching with these people and to see all these bodies advancing across the cobblestones of the smart avenue ... That day we were the ones staring at those bourgeois men and women, we were the ones who had the right to be there and march down the middle of the road, and they had to be quiet and scared. Because we were marching to victory.' What came bursting out at that moment, according to Marion, is a 'physical event produced by unknown emotions, a sense of history being made, combined with something unique'. A historic event.

One of the placards held aloft on the Champs-Élysées since the very beginning of the movement reads: 'Dear bourgeoisie, can we not all live with dignity, please?' A banner puts the same sentiment in starker terms: 'The people are on their knees, death to the bourgeoisie.' Many slogans express bitter anger towards the president: 'The cynics and the lazy have come for the contemptuous and the greedy'; 'Macron, your disdain and arrogance are an insult to France'; 'We'll help you across the street.' Memories come flooding back, accentuating people's sense of being looked down upon. Macron's comment about workers, 'many of them illiterate', things he said about 'nothing people', 'the cynics, the lazy, the extremists' and the certainty he voiced that people only had to 'cross the street' to find a job. In

response, there is an anti-establishment, situationist feel to the avenue: '*Sur les pavés, la rage*' ('On the cobbles, the rage') echoes the May 1968 motto '*Sous les pavés, la plage*' ('Under the cobbles, the beach'); 'We want to pay ISF too' (ISF is the wealth tax); '*Victoire par chaos*' ('Victory through chaos', a pun on '*Victoire par KO*' or 'Victory by a knockout'); 'People and finance don't get on' ... And there is also a furious tag daubed on a luxury store's smashed window: 'We're deducting the ISF at source.' The slogans take aim at the financial industry, the media and the police as the armed wing of the state: 'Media = state propaganda'; 'The banks rule us'; 'Welcome to Teargasistan.' Many call for revolution, sometimes playing on the name of the ruling party, La République en Marche with '*La révolution en marche*' ('The revolution on the move'); 'Elites: optimisation, low taxation, evasion / The people: privations, frustration. Revolution?' One protester, channelling the writer Lautréamont, has smeared 'As beautiful as an impure insurrection' along the Champs. There's nothing pure about this event – that much is undeniable. The rebellion has got out of hand and entered uncharted territory.

These statements by the *gilets jaunes* highlight social deprivation, expressing concerns that are all too frequently reduced to statistics in concrete and tangible terms. 'We are all politicians,' reads one of the vests. Politics isn't the preserve of those who govern; it is a public good, *res publica*, a thing shared. This uprising is all about exposing other forms of violence than the smashed shop windows. The violence of

social contempt and the gulf between the poor and the rich. The violence of the pressure to take any job, crushing any notion of solidarity and sometimes even a person's dignity. The violence of misery at work and on benefits. The brutal culture of competitiveness and management by obedience.

From this moment on the revolt looks beyond simply exercising its power of refusal. All over the country people write lists of demands – sometimes called *cahiers de doléances* after the lists of grievances drawn up in pre-revolutionary France and presented to the Estates General. They call for increases to the minimum wage, basic welfare payments and pensions. They demand a massive public-sector hiring campaign for schools, post offices, hospitals and transport, a vast home-building scheme and penalties for mayors and officials who tolerate people sleeping rough. They catalogue the gigantic sums swallowed up by tax evasion and 'gifts' to investors. They want to abolish the current tax structure by proposing the cancellation of tax rises and the reinstatement of the wealth tax, while also protesting against socially regressive indirect taxes. They challenge many lethal aberrations that are damaging to the environment, from the huge amounts of plastic waste from useless gadgets to planned obsolescence. What is emerging is clearly a blueprint for a fairer, more supportive society.

'Minister, are you planning to destroy the Champs-Élysées?' begins the letter addressed by the member of parliament for the France Insoumise ('France Unbowed') party, François Ruffin, to the minister for culture, Franck Riester. There is a certain irony here: the letter is dated 1 April 2019. The MP's goal is to help save a grassroots work of art. With the help of a few friends a worker in Villeneuve-sur-Lot has built a six-metre lookalike of the Arc de Triomphe from recycled wood. The structure is a memorial to Olivier Daurelle who was crushed to death by a lorry in December 2018 while occupying a roundabout. The *gilets jaunes* of Villeneuve explain that 'We're up against someone who doesn't answer us, doesn't listen to us. So we said to ourselves that we'd put this nice piece of artwork here. It'll make us visible. There have been times this winter at the roundabout when we've doubted. Tough times, difficult times. This helped to keep us going. We lost Olivier. He was one of our leaders, a great guy, a democrat, a pacifist. He was our monument. Everyone listened to him. He was knocked down by a lorry forcing its way through. The driver was in the wrong, but no one's ever really talked about that ...'

The *gilets jaunes* see the arch as a symbol of peaceful protest and a piece of vernacular art, but the prefect of the department has ordered that it be destroyed. At the same time, in Cannet-des-Maures in the Var, a department of Provence, some *gilets jaunes* built another Arc de Triomphe, this one out of around a hundred pallets, a job that took two hundred hours. This monument, too, is demolished – by the company that owns the roundabout, Vinci.

One branch of Fouquet's is planned in Abu Dhabi, but other more modest ones have already opened at Angles in the Gard department in the south, at Valenciennes in the north, both small huts the *gilets jaunes* have named after the famous brasserie. Some of the replicas of the Champs-Élysées

Left top: A demonstrator draped in the French tricolour walks past an advertisement for Lacoste.
Left bottom: Police in riot gear face demonstrators in Paris.

are deadly serious, others are ironic. They mark their distance from the avenue while also appropriating it. Throughout the revolt, some journalists have held up the Arc de Triomphe and Fouquet's incidents as emblematic of a damaged republic. Those same journalists, incidentally, seem not to show any sympathy for the people who have been – literally – blinded during the crackdown. How is it possible to be more outraged by damage to a plaster statue than that to the faces of real women and men, some of them very young, leaving them mutilated for ever? This question will remain unanswered.

IN THE RED AND IN THE ROUND

It is Christmas Eve. The daily papers inform us that in Laval, in western France, the lights 'are in no way inferior to the Champs-Élysées'. I smile, and I'm pleased, although I have my doubts. That evening the avenue is ablaze with light – and that isn't a metaphor. It looks like a forest of scarlet trees: the illuminations are in flames. The Champs want us to see a *vie en rouge*. Colours really have lost their political affiliations. In a cock-up tinged with irony, one of the French Air Force acrobatic team, the Patrouille de France, spat out a trail of red instead of blue during the Bastille Day military parade. And red has been the colour of the Champs since the demonstrations began – the red of shame. Even Fouquet's Yule log is covered in 'bright-red marzipan' this year to mirror the colour of the brasserie's awning. No effort is spared to make Paris worthy of its sobriquet the City of Lights once again. By a quirk of history, the association that organises the Christmas lights on the Champs-Élysées was founded on 11 May 1968. Four days earlier the student movement had taken control of the Champs-Élysées to announce with bravado their radical critique, and

On 19 July 2016, his twenty-fourth birthday, Adama Traoré, a French citizen of Malian descent, died in the Persan barracks in the Val d'Oise after fleeing from an earlier arrest. The gendarmes had stopped him on the street, and Adama, recently released from prison and without an identity card, had run off. The causes of his death are disputed: according to the police, he died of a cardiogenic oedema linked to pre-existing health conditions and the physical stress experienced during his escape; according to his family, the cardiogenic oedema was caused by 'positional asphyxiation caused by prone restraint' – in other words, the arrest technique used by the gendarmes. Since then Adama's older sister, Assa Traoré, has been fighting for truth and justice. In a survey published in the summer of 2020 by the Seine-Saint-Denis authorities, over 80 per cent of those interviewed said they thought ethnicity or skin colour gave rise to discrimination in dealings with the police or at work. Young people aged eighteen to twenty-five perceived to be black or Arab are twenty times more likely to be stopped by the police than their white peers. In the wake of the protests that broke out in the USA following George Floyd's death in 2020, the Comité Adama's struggle gained resonance at a national level and beyond. Tens of thousands of people came out on the streets to protest about police violence, with banners repeating the slogans seen in the USA: 'BLM – Black Lives Matter' and '*Je n'arrive plus a respirer*' ('I can't breathe'), the last words of both Adama and George Floyd.

'Walter Benjamin wrote in *The Arcades Project* that the "mighty seek to secure their position with blood (police), with cunning (fashion), with magic (pomp)". The Champs-Élysées is a concentrate of these three ingredients.'

two days later the general strike began. Rebellion is revealing. It also lifts a corner of the veil obscuring social divisions. Amid all the sparkling splendour it is impossible not to think of everything that remains in the shadows. 'Cover that world that I cannot bear to see,' a modern Molière might remark about society's hypocrisy.

Yet for around a decade now 'roundabout revolutions' (as the British-Israeli architect Eyal Weizman dubbed them in his 2015 book of the same name) have shaken societies whose wheels are usually so well oiled. They have come to demonstrate that the world is not running as smoothly as it might seem. Roundabouts, these banal and practical traffic-management measures, become strategic sites when occupied. Weizman writes that it is like tactical acupuncture: all the roads entering and leaving them are blocked. It just so happens that Place de l'Étoile was the world's first round-about, along with Columbus Circle in New York City. Its designer, Eugène Hénard, an architect for Paris city council, called it a 'turning crossroads' in 1907. The irony of the matter is that a system intended to increase traffic flow has become a place where 'politics is relocated', according to the sociologist Laurent Jeanpierre. Essentially, this echoes the philosopher Jacques Rancière's analysis of what is political: it is not the 'move along, nothing to see here' of the police managing a crowd but conflict and the demand for equality.

Beneath the Place de l'Étoile is a vast unoccupied space that Paris city council now plans to put to good use, perhaps as a huge wine cellar or a luxury shopping centre. In a part of town where every square metre of land is worth a fortune, it seems unthinkable not to wring some money from the basement. It would be impossible just to leave it as it is – the market abhors a vacuum. The only certainty is that it will be converted into something prestigious.

Walter Benjamin wrote in *The Arcades Project* that the 'mighty seek to secure their position with blood (police), with cunning (fashion), with magic (pomp)'. The Champs-Élysées is a concentrate of these three ingredients. No wonder it was targeted. No wonder a popular uprising tried to occupy it. Those who sought to unmask the cunning and defy the 'magic' by showing that the reality was very different sometimes paid the price – the price in blood in the case of those blinded and mutilated. To convey the distress of the struggle to make ends meet, the helplessness of being trapped in a precarious job and poverty's brutal embrace in this nexus of power was a challenge, a unique opportunity, an echo chamber for this struggle for equality. It casts these Elysian Fields in a very different light: behind the façade – a negative of the Champs. ✎

This article is extracted from *«La plus belle avenue du monde»: Une histoire sociale et politique des Champs-Élysées* by Ludivine Bantigny (La Découverte, 2020).

At a private view in Paris.

On Being French and Chinese

TASH AW

French people of Chinese descent in Paris –
one of Europe's largest Asian communities
– have long faced prejudice and violence. But
today a new generation, brought up under
the French school system's cult of *égalité*, is
laying claim to its rightful place in society.

49

On 7 August 2016 Zhang Chaolin, a 49-year-old tailor, was savagely beaten by a group of youths in Aubervilliers, a deprived suburb on the northern outskirts of Paris – the latest in a string of violent aggressions against ethnic Chinese. Like the other victims, he had been targeted because of the widely held belief that members of the Chinese community habitually carry large amounts of cash (and that they are docile and unlikely to fight back; that they are reluctant to report crimes because they are in the country illegally or cannot express themselves properly in French; and even if they do, the police do not take them seriously; or, simply, that the Chinese 'keep themselves to themselves'). As it turned out, Zhang Chaolin only had a packet of cigarettes and some sweets on him. He died as a result of his injuries five days later.

The following year, on 26 March, 56-year-old Liu Shaoyo was preparing dinner for his children in his apartment in the 19th arrondissement in Paris when the police arrived at his home following a call from neighbours (the nature of the complaint remains unclear). The precise sequence of events is disputed: his family insist firmly that he had merely been gutting fish and had answered the door while still holding a pair of kitchen scissors; the police claim that they had acted in self-defence. Either way, they opened fire, killing Liu Shaoyo.

In the aftermath of each man's death, huge demonstrations were held by France's ethnic Chinese, a community traditionally invisible in national discourse and under-represented in public life. I was transfixed by video footage of a crowd of more than fifteen thousand in the Place de la République in 2016 shortly after Chaolin's death on 12 August, protesting against continuing attacks on ethnic Chinese in Paris. Much of what I heard in the speeches that day, as well as in newspaper reports and on social media, felt tragically familiar to me: the cries of a people who felt that they had been ignored by the state. *We work hard, we keep out of trouble, no one gives a damn about us, we have to struggle all by ourselves.* These were the sentiments I grew up with in my ethnic-Chinese family in Malaysia – a sense of frustration and suppressed pain that informed my view of the world.

TASH AW was born in Taipei to Malaysian parents and grew up in Kuala Lumpur before moving to Britain to attend university. He is the author of four critically acclaimed novels, *The Harmony Silk Factory*, *Map of the Invisible World*, *Five Star Billionaire* and *We, the Survivors*, which have variously won the Whitbread First Novel Award, a regional Commonwealth Writers' Prize and twice been longlisted for the Man Booker Prize; they have also been translated into twenty-three languages. His short fiction has won an O. Henry Prize and been published in *A Public Space* and the landmark *Granta 100* among others. *Five Star Billionaire* has recently been optioned for development as a TV series.

> 'The protesters were overwhelmingly young, incredibly vocal and, in some instances, willing to resort to violent action.'

But there was also something totally foreign to me about these protests: the open dissent. Pushing back against hierarchy and authority. The protesters were overwhelmingly young, incredibly vocal and, in some instances, willing to resort to violent action – the very opposite of how overseas Chinese communities, the centuries-old immigrants known as *huaqiao*, have traditionally behaved. In short, the demonstrations seemed to be distinctly French.

I had been as surprised as most people to learn that France has the largest ethnic-Chinese population in Europe. In a country where race-based statistics sit uneasily with the notion of *égalité* and French citizenship, it's often difficult to find accurate figures, although most estimates suggest a population of at least 600,000–700,000, more than double that of the United Kingdom.

There were other surprises, too. In France, where I have travelled and lived on and off for more than fifteen years, I have always taken the French habit of calling anyone of East or Southeast Asian appearance '*chinois*' as a laziness bordering on casual racism, particularly since France is home to large Vietnamese and Cambodian communities who arrived in the country in great numbers following the wars in the former French colonies in the 1970s. But as I got to know members of the various Asian communities in Paris, I discovered that I had been guilty of overlooking a fact that should have been obvious to me, of all people: that the overwhelming majority of Cambodians and Vietnamese in France are

of Chinese descent. That is to say, like me, they come from Southeast Asian Chinese families – families who had already been immigrants in their home countries before moving to Europe and for whom being an outsider is integral to their sense of identity. Their languages – Cantonese and Teochew – are those I have lived with my whole life.

I learned, too, of the vast distinctions within the Chinese community, principally between the Southeast Asians and the huge numbers of newer immigrants from the mainland, overwhelmingly from the factory-port city of Wenzhou.

I met the people who had organised the most visible of the demonstrations. They have since mobilised themselves into a group that promotes not just political but social and cultural change – the Association of Young Chinese of France, one of the most notable of the many Asian action groups that are being established in the country. Over the course of many months we've walked through the Asian neighbourhoods of Paris, shared meals and become friends over the messy issue of mixed identity. They've spoken about what it means to be French and Chinese.

93: CROSSROADS
The suburbs of Aubervilliers and Pantin lie just beyond the north-eastern corner of the Périphérique, part of the department of Seine-Saint-Denis, notorious in the French public imagination for its perceived levels of crime and deprivation and known colloquially as 'le neuf-trois' after its departmental number. At

This 2012 map, published by Emmanuel Vigneron, uses standardised mortality ratios – which compare observed deaths with expected deaths in a population (0.7 at Port-Royal, 1.3 at Stade de France) – to show health inequalities along the RER B, an eighty-kilometre suburban railway line that crosses the Paris region. The risk of dying in any given year increases by 82 per cent in the space of a fifteen-minute train ride from a wealthy neighbourhood (Port-Royal) to a more deprived area (Stade de France).

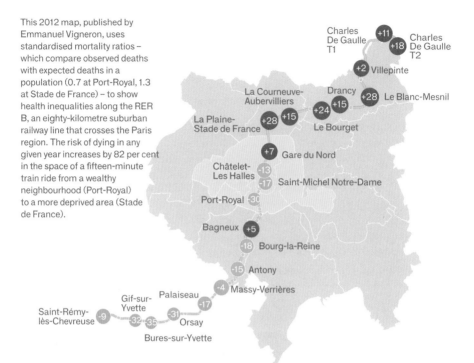

'LES MIS' OF THE 93

The department of Seine-Saint-Denis, to the north-east of Paris, has a special relationship with the cinema. In the early 20th century it was where Georges Méliès and Charles Pathé set up their film studios. Today it is home to the Cité du Cinéma studio complex, a project launched and financed by the director Luc Besson in the early 2000s. But the 93 is more famous as the setting for some of the best-known French films, beginning in 1995 with *La Haine*, directed by Mathieu Kassovitz. While Kassovitz hails from central Paris, Ladj Ly, director of the more recent *Les Misérables*, was born in Mali and raised in Montfermeil, the home of Victor Hugo's original *misérables* and the location for his film. Ly became the first black director to win a César for best film. These productions emphasise the harshest realities of the department, which, particularly since the 2005 *banlieue* riots, has been synonymous with urban poverty and inequality, as is further illustrated by its higher incidence of Covid-19 than the rest of the country. The 93 is the department with the highest unemployment rate in the whole of France (with levels of 50 per cent among young people). It is also the department with the highest concentration of immigrants (two-thirds of the children born in 2015 had at least one parent born abroad), many of them from the former colonies of North and West Africa. This is what Ly explores in his film: police violence, institutional racism, a chronic housing crisis and a lack of prospects for the youth, who are drawn to crime and radical Islam. Football and hip-hop provide a way out, as was the case for Aya Nakamura, a Malian singer with French citizenship raised in the 93, whose hit 'Djadja' climbed the charts around the world in 2018.

Quatre Chemins, the crossroads that form the heart of the neighbourhood, the first building I see when I emerge from the Métro bears a sign that reads HÔTEL À LA JOURNÉE / €53 LA NUIT. *People hurry along the streets, as if to and from work, in contrast to the more bourgeois districts of Paris, which are already empty now that the summer holidays are here.*

Rui, aged thirty-two:

'I arrived in France in 1995, when I was seven and a half. My parents had already been here for some years, having arrived in Europe from Wenzhou, in the south of China. They had papers for Italy but had come to France illegally, so when I arrived I was an illegal, too. One of my earliest memories of my childhood in France was of my father not returning home one night and my mother telling me that he'd been arrested by the police for not having the right papers. He didn't come home for three days. Eventually he was released – they couldn't prove anything, so he was free to come home, but we lived with that fear all the time. It was exhausting.

'Before we got our papers, I lived constantly with my father's shame – the shame of being a poor clandestine. We lived entirely within the Chinese community, that is to say, entirely within the Wenzhou community. Some had papers, many didn't. There was a very distinct hierarchy, a division between those who were legal and those who weren't. In those early days, not so many of us had a passport, and if you got married to a French citizen it was like getting married to Bill Gates or Hillary Clinton – the most privileged thing in the world!

'My father was the opposite end of this spectrum. He worked in the lowest of shitty jobs, as a *plongeur* in Chinese restaurants – that sort of thing. I could feel his shame at being an illegal immigrant every time he talked to anyone. I could hear it in his voice – he felt crushed by the world. *Why?* I asked myself. Why do we have to live with this shame? I would go home at night and cry myself to sleep. Because they were illegals, my parents were forced to accept their position at the bottom of the ladder, and their inferiority complex coloured their experience of life, even at that age.

'Every single time they went out, my parents would take me along with them. "In France the police won't arrest us if we have a child with us," they used to say. Even at that age, I knew that I was being used as a human shield. I'd be playing or reading quietly at home and suddenly my parents would say, "We need to go out." I never had any time for myself. Sometimes I feel as though I had my childhood taken away from me, confiscated against my will.

'People don't stay in Quatre Chemins long. As soon as they have a decent job and some money, they move to a better neighbourhood. Those who stay aren't so lucky. We were here for many years, just up the road on the Pantin side of the crossroads. Down there, just a couple of hundred metres away, was where Zhang Chaolin was attacked. There's been a lot of talk in recent years about the violence in Aubervilliers and Pantin, but in truth it's always been difficult here, there have always been aggressions, robberies, fights. [*As if on cue, at our very first meeting in a café in the heart of Quatre Chemins, a fight suddenly breaks out between the Wenzhounese café owner and a man who had walked in off the street, an altercation which spills out on to the pavement and results in the appearance of the police in just a few minutes.*] This is where the Chinese community live, but they mostly work on the other side of Aubervilliers, where they run wholesale businesses, mainly of clothes, shoes and bags. It's a barren area,

> **"'I realise that a large part of the shame was what we were going to tell our family back in China. We had left to build better lives for ourselves in France, but here we were, worse off than before.'"**

very harsh, and it's on the way to and from work that they've been getting attacked and robbed. What you hear about Chinese people feeling scared and not wanting to go out unless they're in groups – it's true. But look around you: you can see we also have ordinary lives in a very mixed community.

'It looked as if our lives were condemned to forever being lived in the shadows, and my parents were ready to abandon their French dream and return to Italy. But then, in 1997 a *coup de théâtre*, and suddenly our fortunes were transformed. Jacques Chirac, who was president at the time, decided to call fresh legislative elections because he believed they would reinforce the right and destroy the left. But the plan backfired, and instead it was the left who won the elections and proceeded to put in place a programme of regularisation for people who'd lived without papers for many years in the country. All of a sudden we became normal members of society, and that changed everything for us: the kinds of jobs my parents were suddenly eligible for, the way they could hold their heads up in public, even my behaviour at school. I felt confident, I felt the same as everyone else. It's not as if we became rich or anything, but almost overnight we felt as if life held possibilities for us. I remember the day we got our papers, my mother took me to a restaurant for the first time – a simple Vietnamese place where we had pho. It felt like such a luxury.

'Now that I have a good job – I work in real estate, I have a decent income and I own a nice apartment – I sometimes think back to those days of poverty, when we were illegal and my family had no money, no possibility of earning money or of getting any social security. And I realise that a large part of the shame was what we were going to tell our family back in China. We had left to build better lives for ourselves in France, but here we were, worse off than before. We were trapped in a sort of double prison: by poverty in Europe and by China and its expectations of us.

'After I became a full French citizen at the age of eighteen, I started to think more deeply about my identity – about what it meant to be French and also Chinese. By that time I and all my cousins and friends, people who'd been brought up or even born in France, had experienced racism in France – from casual insults, people mocking our accents or more serious incidents like being robbed because we were seen as weak and docile. And then, during the Beijing Olympics, we saw how the French media talked about China and *the Chinese*, as if we were one kind of people, who acted in the same way, always in the image of the Communist Party. That got me really mad, so together with other

Right: Rui in Aubervilliers.

After finishing school, French students can enrol at a university, which are generally public institutions, and around three-fifths of the 2.7 million students choose this route. But there is also another option: the *grandes écoles*, public or private higher-education institutions with highly selective admission requirements that are separate and parallel to the university system. To secure a place most students attend two years of preparatory classes or enrol after two or three years at university (so-called 'parallel admission', which is open to students from all across Europe). Some studies suggest that 90 per cent of graduates from the *grandes écoles* find a job within six months, and within twelve they are all in employment. They form the country's public and private elite: four of the last six presidents graduated from the *grande école* for administration (ENA) – however, Macron, himself an '*énarque*', has announced that the school is to close. The system has given France world-class engineering, economics and mathematics schools that nevertheless struggle to attract talent from abroad: the fragmentation of the system prevents individual universities, research institutes or *grandes écoles* from reaching the highest echelons in international rankings. Since the 2000s France has pursued a policy of 'university grouping' to create clusters combining various institutions. The flagship is Paris-Saclay University, which was officially established in 2019 and immediately entered the global ranking in fourteenth place, the only European institution to buck the trend of Anglo-American dominance.

friends like me – young Chinese people who considered France their only home – I formed the Association of Young Chinese of France. I was at university at the time, at Paris Dauphine, and reading Marx and Bourdieu – people who helped me make sense of my childhood, of the way my parents' experience conditioned mine. I wanted to change things – for me and also for them.

'When Zhang Chaolin was in hospital and everyone knew he was going to die, I knew I had to do something. Together with a few other young people, we made plans for a huge demonstration that we would put into action the moment he died. When I saw all those people gathered for the demonstration outside the *mairie* of the 19th arrondissement, I felt elated – as if change was finally happening.

'What happened at the demonstration to mark Liu Shaoyo's death was even more remarkable. The elders of the Chinese community had organised a formal event, full of boring speeches that tried to appease everyone. Everything was expressed in neutral language, with typical Chinese politesse. Not that many people were present. Then, not long before proceedings were due to wrap up, a huge swathe of protesters dressed in black descended towards the Place de la République, shouting slogans against the establishment. All of them were young Chinese people, angry with the inaction of the older generation. They wanted change, they wanted it urgently. All of it was calculated to make the elders lose face, to show how powerless and pointless they were. It was exhilarating to see that mass of young people trying to wrest control from their elders.

'For me, the demonstrations were a form of revenge. For the humiliation that my parents experienced. That I've experienced. The humiliation of being rendered invisible, of not being listened to. The humiliation that Chinese people go through every time they are aggressed in the street, which is a continuation of the marginalisation my parents lived through.

'But, above all, these protests, this spirit of revolution – this is what makes me French. In Chinese culture, as you and I both know all too well, we're trained to be obedient, to respect our elders and hierarchy in general. In France it's the reverse. You become integrated from the moment you feel able to criticise, especially if you criticise the state and the government. It's a particularly French quality, almost a disease, I would say! In this country, we are French, we are required to be French, and this requires a very special mentality. For Chinese-French people it's not the same as Chinese-Italians or Chinese-Spanish, who are always thinking they will never be fully integrated and will probably go back to China in ten years' time. We think of our children and grandchildren living normal lives in this country, so we need to change things. I have a way of thinking which I feel defines a French person: I believe that the government can always, always, be changed. I believe in the power of revolution to change our lives.'

13: SOUTHEAST ASIA

The southern end of Paris's 13th arrondissement is home to the city's largest and longest-established Asian community, composed principally of families who fled the civil wars in Cambodia, Vietnam and Laos, arriving in France in large numbers after the fall of Saigon and Phnom Penh in 1975. The heart of Chinatown is concentrated around the famous residential tower blocks known as Les Olympiades, completed in the mid-1970s – the first homes to be occupied by the families arriving from Southeast Asia.

Laëtitia, aged twenty-five:

'One of the things my parents often used to say in reprimanding me was "*Tu es devenue trop française*" – you've become too French. Whenever they were angry they also used the term "*ang mo kia*", which was not intended as a compliment [*'white kid' in many of the dialects of southern China, shorthand for rude, rebellious behaviour, Western values being, of course, the antithesis of harmony, both within the family and in society*]. I think it came from a frustration that we, their children, had very little idea of what they went through so that we could grow up with an idea of being French and only French. But then again, they never spoke of their lives before coming to France or their difficult journeys here, so it's no surprise that most of us only have a single French identity.

'My parents are Sino-Cambodian, that is to say, ethnic Chinese Teochews from Chaozhou who were born or grew up in Cambodia with a dual identity, both Chinese and Cambodian. During the war, just before the country fell to the Khmer Rouge, they were forced to flee, abandoning everything they had and, in some cases, even members of their own family. They spent the whole of the war trapped in camps on the Thai border. During that

'"French identity is an incredibly powerful idea. Being French is a notion that is inculcated within us from the earliest days at primary school, and it's a really attractive principle: a project of assimilation to push aside cultural origins to create one single nationality, one people."'

time, who knows what kind of horrors they witnessed? I can understand why they wouldn't want to talk about it. Like many Cambodians, their lives had been all right over there – they ran shops and small businesses. Then, almost overnight: the war, the nightmare of departure and finally France.

'Despite my parents' silence, I knew that they survived unspeakable brutality in Cambodia, and this knowledge is something unspoken that I carry within me, affecting the way I feel about France. Intellectually, I can understand why the *gilets jaunes* are protesting, I'm French after all. I have the tendency to question the way other French people do. But when you know that your parents have survived one of the greatest genocides the world has ever seen, everything becomes relative. When people talk of *life's great problems* being the price of petrol and only being able to go to a restaurant once a week or only having one holiday a year, we can't feel fully invested in these arguments even if we understand them. My parents ran a restaurant when I was a child, and I can't remember them ever taking a holiday. That's why they pushed me to have a life where I could make choices and have greater agency than them.

'As a rule, I don't think you'll find many French people from Southeast Asian Chinese families, that is to say Cambodian or Vietnamese, who are passionate about the right to take to the streets. We don't take the attitude that "the government has to do everything for me". Even back in Cambodia and Vietnam, our families were already outsiders. We didn't benefit from any structural help then, we didn't come from the dominant class in those countries, we didn't feel we had the right to demand anything. We knew we had to fend for ourselves. Even though the overwhelming majority of Asians of my generation would consider themselves French and only French, I don't know anyone who relies on state subsidies to live – two generations of French citizenship are not enough to change the embedded mentality of self-sufficiency.

'French identity is an incredibly powerful idea. Being French is a notion that is inculcated within us from the earliest days at primary school, and it's a really attractive principle: a project of assimilation to push aside cultural origins to create one single nationality, one people. But the problem is that differences persist, and as my teenage years went by I suddenly began to think there's something missing, some part of myself that is not acknowledged, and that's when I began to interrogate the Chinese part of myself and learn how to be culturally Chinese as well as French.

'"From what I see in my circle of friends, ethnic Chinese are far more likely to reject their Chineseness than a *Maghrebin* their Arabness. I'm not sure why – maybe it's to do with the silence that exists within many families."'

'You can see the problems in the unacknowledged differences in culture and race when you look at the aggression against Chinese people in certain parts of Paris. Asian and North African communities live in tough conditions and have come to think about each other in negative stereotypes. We can't speak about it along racial lines because to do so is taboo, totally contrary to the ideas of the Republic, of *égalité* and so on. But the problems exist.

'The rise of China has been complicated for us. Before that, no one really noticed Asian people – we just got on with our lives in a nearly invisible way. Then I began to hear overtly racist comments like, *Chinese spit everywhere, they're filthy, they're money launderers*. The most negative phase was in 2008–9, during the Beijing Olympics, when suddenly the old "Yellow Peril" fears were everywhere. All the time we had newspaper stories entitled "China: Conquering the World". There were TV programmes like *Envoyé spécial*, which killed Chinese delicatessens almost overnight by screening "exposés" on hygiene standards. My parents ran one of those delis, so I should know.

'I guess that's why many people from my community say that they are Cambodian or Vietnamese, to distance themselves from associations with the mainland and from the newer immigrants from Wenzhou, who've only been in France for twenty years or so. We've been here since the 1970s, and already there's a sense within our communities of being more French than they are, more part of the community, which gives us a sense of superiority. The things we say about them echo what the rest of France say about us: that they work really hard, they're prepared to work very long hours for next to nothing, they keep themselves to themselves and so on. We're used to being the model immigrants, but there are newer versions of ourselves, and we pass judgements on them. Maybe that's a sign of belonging to French society.'

Daniel, aged twenty-seven:
'I would say that among all my Asian friends, I'm in the minority of those who are comfortable with being both Asian and French. A very small number, I guess those who've been victims of consistent racism, choose to reject their French identity, but the vast majority are more comfortable inhabiting only a French identity and are prepared to reject any sense of Asianness if it clashes with feeling French.

'From what I see in my circle of friends, ethnic Chinese are far more likely to reject their Chineseness than a *Maghrebin* their Arabness. I'm not sure why – maybe it's to do with the silence that exists within many families, particularly those from Vietnam and Cambodia, the lack of knowledge about our histories. We're not connected

Right: Daniel exiting the Métro.

The first Chinese immigrants arrived in Paris around the beginning of the 20th century, when students, journalists and a few craftsmen moved into the area around the Gare de Lyon. In the 1920s Zhou Enlai, who would become the first premier of the People's Republic of China, spent time there, as did Deng Xiaoping, the pioneer of the country's economic reforms after Mao's death. The first Chinese restaurant, the Empire Céleste, opened in 1912; it is still trading in the Rue Royer-Collard. In the inter-war period the Chinese community was joined by specialist leather workers and established a presence in the 3rd arrondissement in what is the oldest but now the smallest Chinatown in Paris. After the closure of China's borders in 1949 new sources of Asian immigration emerged. In the 1970s Vietnamese, Cambodians and Laotians fleeing communist regimes established themselves in the 13th, in the 'Choisy Triangle', where they were later replaced by ethnic-Chinese immigrants from Southeast Asia and, from the 1980s, from China itself. With a population of fifty thousand they occupy the largest Asian district in Europe, recognisable not from its architecture (the pagoda roofs of Les Olympiades housing complex were already there) but from the shops, like the ubiquitous Tang Frères and Paristore supermarkets. There is another large but less visible Asian community in Belleville, in the 10th. Outside the city are Marne-la-Vallée, France's second largest Chinese community after its Parisian counterpart, and the textile industry 'golden triangle' of Aubervilliers, now the base for the import–export trade with China, with vast wholesale business centres such as the Fashion Business Center, the largest in Europe, where 310 wholesalers occupy more than 55,000 square metres.

to our non-French past the way Arabs and Africans are. They tend to have extended families back in Ivory Coast or Morocco or Algeria who provide them with a link to their cultures, their languages. We don't have that – there's no one back in Vietnam who can give me that sense of belonging to another culture. In any case, there's a complication, because my family are ethnic Chinese who speak Cantonese, so which is my "other" culture?

'There's a question of visibility, too. Black Africans and North Africans are represented in public life – in sports, music and pop culture in general – whereas we are almost totally absent. That means that it's more difficult for us to identify role models.

'Another pressure is that our parents often live life through us. Their aspirations, all the things they weren't able to achieve because they arrived in France too late in life, traumatised and with very little money, they invest in us. Part of that means figuring out how to live in France. Many of us have experience of being interpreters for our parents even when we were very small. So, of course, it's natural we end up behaving like models of French society.

'We don't recognise ourselves in French history, which is one of the most important subjects at school, because this is a country that has a long and rich history. We absorb all the lessons on French heroes such as Jeanne d'Arc, Charlemagne, Clovis. It's one single version of history, one story, which everyone, even children of immigrant families, is obliged to accept as their own. Even though I tried to feel that it was my story, I couldn't help feeling a bit detached from it. To accept that version of history as my only heritage felt false – it was a story that rendered us invisible. Coupled with the misleading stereotypes elsewhere, it felt to me that our fate in society was either

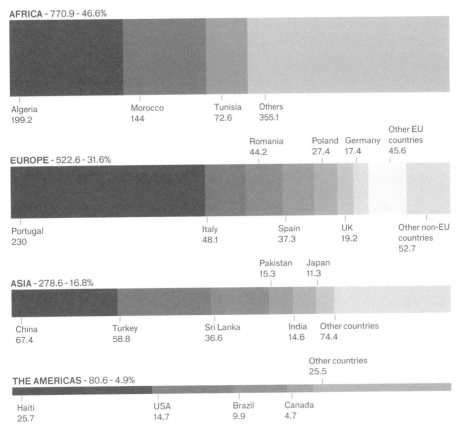

Thousands of people

AFRICA - 770.9 - 46.6%

Algeria	Morocco	Tunisia	Others
199.2	144	72.6	355.1

EUROPE - 522.6 - 31.6%

| Portugal | | Italy | | Spain | | Romania | Poland | Germany | Other EU countries |
| 230 | | 48.1 | | 37.3 | | 44.2 | 27.4 | 17.4 | 45.6 |

| | | | | | UK | | Other non-EU countries |
| | | | | | 19.2 | | 52.7 |

ASIA - 278.6 - 16.8%

| China | Turkey | Sri Lanka | India | Pakistan | Japan | Other countries |
| 67.4 | 58.8 | 36.6 | 14.6 | 15.3 | 11.3 | 74.4 |

THE AMERICAS - 80.6 - 4.9%

| Haiti | USA | Brazil | Canada | Other countries |
| 25.7 | 14.7 | 9.9 | 4.7 | 25.5 |

SOURCE: INSEE

not to be talked about or to be talked about inaccurately.

'We were taught next to nothing about Vietnam, which was after all one of France's most important colonies for a hundred years. Colonial history – France's relationship with countries that would provide large numbers of its minority populations – wasn't taught much at school, which was a shame. I remember the kids of Algerian origin being very interested in lessons on the war in Algeria. They felt as if it spoke of them, that the whole class was learning about them and their past, where their parents came from, why they were French, how they were French. There was nothing for us, but in some ways that's natural. Algeria represents a greater presence in

THE PASSENGER Tash Aw

the French imagination than Vietnam, even if that relationship is problematic. You have to understand, we grow up with the notion that all of us are French – that is the whole point of our history lessons, to give us one single shared identity. I get that. But isn't it more important to learn why we are so diverse? We're all French, but these days there are so many different ways of being French. I'd have loved to have learned more about the histories of the different communities in France – their music, art, language. I'd also have liked to learn about the history of racism, rather than have to figure it all out myself.'

11: GENTRIFICATION
Boulevard Voltaire is just a fifteen-minute walk from the Place de la Bastille and its concentration of hip bars and restaurants, yet it feels much more down at heel. Most of the shops sell clothing, but there are no customers in them; they have names like Veti Style, Lucky Men and Bella. Many other shop lots are closed and available to rent.

Emma, aged nineteen:
'Until I was in my mid-teens I never had any Chinese friends. In fact, I made a point not to hang out with other Chinese kids. I had only white, Arab or black friends – I was born here and wanted to show how French I was. But around sixteen, seventeen I started to change. I'd had conversations with my parents, who'd come to France from Wenzhou when they were young. "No matter how you feel inside," my father told me, "when the world looks at you, they see a Chinese person." It was around that time, too, that I began to realise that all

Left: Emma checking her phone.

the things I'd accepted as normal – people mocking Chinese accents to my face, even though I speak just like any other French person, casual comments sexualising Asian women and desexualising Asian men – were micro-aggressions, and that I had to embrace my culture instead of rejecting it.

'My parents ran a *bar-tabac* towards the Oberkampf side of the 11th arrondissement. I wanted to do what bourgeois white-French kids do, so I applied to Sciences Po, one of the most prestigious of the country's *grandes écoles*. Few people in my community thought it was worth it – they couldn't imagine it possible for me to pursue a career in human or social sciences, and definitely not in politics. There aren't any statistics on how many Asians there are at Sciences Po, but just from my own observations there are fewer than ten per year, which means thirty in the entire school. It's not like in the US, where Asians are a very visible presence on every major college campus – our elite schools still feel quite foreign to us. Maybe in the more science-based schools there might be more Asians, but personally I really don't know any. If you look at schools like École Normale Supérieure, which require you to have amassed great cultural knowledge by the time you're eighteen or twenty, the figure is probably zero.

'Whatever the real situation, the general impression within the Chinese community is that the most exclusive schools are bastions that we'd have difficulty gaining access to, so when I got in it was a really, really big achievement. Things are changing now, but not as fast as you'd imagine. In the French imagination Asians are studious and conscientious, but if that were true, we would be much more visible in the *grandes écoles*, which are, after all, the standard bearers of French education.' ✍

Defying
the Stars

Tommaso Melilli shelling beans
for the evening's menu.

This is the story of the neo-bistro,
a phenomenon that changed
the face of Parisian society and
its nightlife. By challenging the
dominance of the *Michelin Guide*
star system they transformed the
capital's gastronomic landscape and
brought haute cuisine to the tables
of neighbourhood restaurants.

TOMMASO MELILLI
Translated by Lucy Rand

Paris, 17 March 1791: the revolutionary National Constituent Assembly approves the abolition of the guilds and their archaic privileges, including the tough restrictions that impeded merchants from selling whatever they wanted, wherever they wanted. Up to this point it was absolutely forbidden to serve, say, a cup of coffee in the same establishment as a glass of wine. Restaurants had already been around for decades, but this day saw the birth of what the writer Adam Gopnik calls the Sancho Panza of French culinary history: *le bistrot*. It doesn't take a genius to work out the advantages of being able to consume (and alternate between) alcohol and caffeine under the same roof: the former is a relaxant that loosens the tongue, while the latter is a stimulant that produces lucidity and alertness. The combination of these two liquids swirling around in the same stomach can make an evening feel intriguing and interminable, just as one expects from Paris.

In France, almost all the important events of the subsequent two centuries began at the table of either a restaurant or a bistro. Political, economic and social decisions, declarations of war and treaties of peace started and finished at the table of a restaurant because it was there that the most austere souls and refined minds chose to unwind. Everything else, however, took place in the bistro, where the food was simple and the wine cheap and abundant: the drafting of books, the great film scripts, meetings between extraordinary men and women who didn't yet know it, free love and heartbreak.

*

Two centuries later, at the end of the 1990s, the dominance of French cuisine is universally considered to be at crisis point – well, almost universally; the only ones who haven't realised it yet are the French, notably the top chefs. France's political influence is at an all-time low, and culinary culture, in tandem, is moving away from French opulence and towards shifting international developments: molecular cuisine, insects, roots, the rediscovery of 'nose-to-tail' eating (and therefore offal), the first steps of Nordic cuisine. The French elite is used to thinking that the best restaurants in the world are all found in the arrondissements circling the Eiffel Tower, and they carefully skirt around any questioning of that. These star-spangled restaurants, which often serve as shop windows for the large luxury hotels (the so-called *palaces*), are still serving the same over-complicated dishes they were thirty years before: lobster, foie gras, tiny little birds drowned in cognac, caviar, truffles and porcini in every season, all encased in fifty shades of butter.

International critics, especially the Americans and the British, have simply

TOMMASO MELILLI is a chef and writer who lived and worked in Paris between 2009 and 2018. In 2015 he started the column 'Tovagliette' ('Place Mats') in the magazine *Rivista Studio* in which recipes feature alongside memories and discussions on culture and customs. These spill over into his column 'Pentole e parole' ('Pots and Words') in the weekly supplement *Il Venerdì di Repubblica*, and in *Slate* magazine he writes about his experiences as an Italian chef in France. His first book, *Spaghetti wars: Journal du front des identités culinaires*, came out in French in 2018 (Nouriturfu). After returning to Italy he travelled throughout the country, kitchen by kitchen, writing about his experiences in the book *I conti con l'oste* (Einaudi, 2020), which was also published in French in 2021 by Stock as *L'écume des pâtes: À la recherche de la vraie cuisine italienne*.

> 'There will be no printed menu, as the kitchens are too small ... In its place is a fixed-price tasting menu, a carte blanche, that changes daily.'

stopped going to these places. The clientele now consists of upper-middle-class French, a scattering of the *nouveaux riches* and a large helping of Asian, Russian and Middle Eastern tourists who book tables at these places because they've been told they are the most expensive: deal done. The apprentices of these top chefs, whose sixty-hour weeks sustain the *palaces* of the Rive Gauche, have had enough of shoring up businesses in a state of perdition with their hard labour, and they're starting to make some strange choices. Some are French and have never left the country, having been in the kitchen since the age of sixteen, but others are Italian, Swedish, Spanish, and they came to work in Paris because they were part of the first generation of young Europeans for whom living abroad was an inalienable right. They all trained in the capital's great kitchens, even if only for a few months (they learn fast). They're destined to become the best chefs of their generation, and they'll soon find themselves at the helm of some luxury restaurant or other chasing the highly sought-after stars awarded by the *Michelin Guide* – first one, then two and, maybe one day, a third – after which, so they've been told, the money will start to roll in, and lots of it: consultancy contracts worth millions for hotels in the UAE and honours from the Président de la République. But these are really the aspirations of their parents and their teachers, and the promising young chefs have other dreams they want to follow, gardens they want to cultivate, and they're not bothered if their establishments are small and a tad ramshackle.

They give up their prestigious positions in the kitchens of the grand hotels and starry restaurants, scrape together a little money from here and there and open tiny bars with broken kitchens and furnished with mismatched chairs.

The thing they're most sick of is working in stuffy Rive Gauche Paris where the nightlife is non-existent and, because they're underused, there are long walks between Métro stations: anyone living there is likely to own at least one limo and probably has a chauffeur.

They open bars in the neighbourhoods in which they live alongside their cosmopolitan peers. The city is cut in two by the Seine, and the two halves are defined by the Right Bank and the Left, as you face downstream. At the end of the 1990s it's almost too easy to joke about the fact that la Droite/Right Bank and la Gauche/Left Bank in Paris have been flipped: the north (Rive Droite) is multi-ethnic, fluid, creative and progressive, while the south (Rive Gauche) is old, white, a little bit Catholic, and its inhabitants spend their days pottering about maintaining the status quo.

*

This new generation may be pioneering the garage bistro, but that doesn't mean they're forgetting their international culinary ambitions: they are convinced that they can cook haute cuisine in these tiny local bars and that, in some ways, they'll do it even better than their teachers in the big hotel kitchens. Compromises must be made, naturally, but they are soon turned, in true entrepreneurial spirit,

There are a number of myths that seek to explain the origin of the restaurant as we know it, and the most commonly cited claims that it was established during the French Revolution. As the noble families were stripped of their properties (and sometimes their heads), all the best court chefs found themselves unemployed. Very talented but without a franc to their names, they knew they could do something good but no longer knew who to do it for – so they had to find their public. And so, like today's start-ups, they launched an entirely new concept: the modern restaurant. It's a nice story, but it didn't happen quite that way. Restaurants were indeed a Parisian invention, but it was actually a little while before the French Revolution and for one simple reason: there was a need for them. The European bourgeoisie, especially in France, felt the need for a new type of establishment, one open to all – or almost all – that was pleasant enough and not expensive and was governed by few rules. It has always been important to have a place to meet strangers in a context where it is acceptable to strike up a conversation (the absence of which has been acutely felt during Covid-19 lockdowns). It is essential for work, for business, for conversation, to keep the more casual of our friendships afloat and – above all – it is vital in the pursuit of love. Restaurants were invented because people needed a place to go on a date and decide whether or not to make love afterwards. The very idea of a date is largely inconceivable without the restaurant. (TM)

into advantages: there will be no printed menu, as the kitchens are too small and they can't afford to buy expensive produce that may not be sold. In its place is a fixed-price tasting menu, a carte blanche, that changes daily based on what comes in or what the chefs can get their hands on, because suppliers aren't always willing to deliver to these funny little establishments. The chefs themselves can now be found wandering around the markets or swinging by the Middle Eastern or Chinese *épicerie* with a wooden crate fixed to the back of a bashed-up moped. And if you walk past one of these eateries in the afternoon you'll likely find the chef sitting outside shelling beans with a bottle of beer. (Meanwhile, for a whole host of reasons linked to the needs of the intercontinental clientele, the majority of the generic starred restaurants in France change their menus no more than twice a year. There are just two seasons: autumn for truffles and fungi and a sort of middle ground between spring and summer, where for six months asparagus and tomatoes have to be available whatever the cost.)

In terms of decor, it's clear from day one that there will be no place for the fussiness to which the starred restaurants are so attached. No more tablecloths or embroidered napkins, goodbye silverware, and, in place of those oh-so-awkward designer dinner services that resembled one of Calatrava's bridges but no one ever really liked, supper will now be served on flower-rimmed crockery sourced at a flea market or a garage sale. Now, twenty years on, it's all quite normal, and we might even be starting to tire of all the shabby-chic, but in 1999 you'd have been pretty surprised to have your €40 ($50) menu served on plates your grandmother used to own, and people found it hard to take it seriously. These choices were all a necessary part of lowering the overheads, but, once again, necessity quickly turns to virtue: it goes without saying that these young chefs found the ornate furnishings of the grand restaurants vulgar and garish, but, as it transpired, so did their customers.

*

Back in the 1990s the American journalist David Brooks came up with one of the most incisive social categories of recent years: *les bobos*, a portmanteau of *bourgeois bohème*. The term never really took off in the US, but it was adopted eagerly by the French: it sounds rather disparaging, but *bobos* are always the *others*, the artsy, creative, tech-savvy new French bourgeois who rent or buy cheap apartments on the Rive Droite and who find the old guard on the other side of the river insufferable.

Among the diners who frequented these eateries in Belleville, Oberkampf and Bastille back then was Sébastien Demorand, a jolly food journalist with the face of a fisherman. He was in his thirties at the time (he passed away in January 2020

after a nasty illness), and one evening, perhaps after coming home from Aux Deux Amis, undoubtedly a little tipsy, he declared that he had come up with a name for this new type of eatery. Knowing him, he probably climbed on to a chair and announced it to the whole room. He never wrote it down anywhere himself – and it is one of those stories where many claim to have witnessed an event but which was never properly chronicled – but from that day forward this thing had a name, and it was called *bistronomie*: high-end gastronomy served in a bistro.

Like most things that happen in Paris, it was also a revolution in style: the waiters and waitresses in these neo-bistros were young and free to come to work in their favourite shirts or with stubble on their chins. This parity between staff and customer sent out a very clear message: I am serving you, but I am the same as you.

*

In 2009, when I moved to Paris, *bistronomie* was in full swing. I was twenty, and these long-haired, bearded chefs were rock stars to me. They weren't wearing whites and tall, pleated hats; they worked in T-shirts and trainers, all sporting the same tatty navy-blue apron. I'll be damned if I could ever find out where you could get hold of those aprons; I'd looked everywhere, because I'd decided by that time to become a young chef, just like them. And, hey, while the habit does not make the monk, if you're the only monk dressed differently from the others, people notice.

A few years earlier, in the year 2000, Alexandre Cammas, a young writer for a magazine that no longer exists, had proposed to his editor and mentor that they publish a supplement on Paris's restaurants, a sort of guide to 'authentic' places to eat. One year later it had become

'Like most things that happen in Paris, *bistronomie* was also a revolution in style: the waiters and waitresses in these neo-bistros were young and free to came to work in their favourite shirts or with stubble on their chins.'

a magazine and a website and would later have an app: *Le Fooding*.

Establishing a food guide in the francophone world means going head to head with the elephant in the room: the *Michelin Guide*. Alexandre Cammas says there was no deliberate attempt to foster competition between the two guides, but that's hard to believe, because *Le Fooding* was immediately perceived to be the arch enemy of the guide to the stars. A couple of decades on, *Le Fooding* is *the* authority on the Parisian culinary scene: its writers review bars, restaurants, pizzerias and kebab shops, and on being reviewed these places, without fail, see a queue around the block for the next two weeks. Over the last few years it seems the clientele of the Michelin-starred restaurants have resigned themselves to venturing out in an Uber – or being driven by their chauffeurs – into the hinterlands, the new place to be seen. While Paris's art scene has become somewhat static and conservative, for younger chefs the city has become the centre of the universe.

The *Michelin Guide* relies on symbols: forks, hats and stars. *Le Fooding* uses no such hierarchies but instead a series of tags and keywords that describe each eatery. They're categories I've never seen in any other guide and ones that I find pleasingly vague, evocative and extremely effective. For example: 'so good', 'kid friendly', 'good vibes', 'dining solo', 'late-night hunger', 'anti-depressant', 'terrace', 'hurts so good', 'brunch' and 'see and be seen'. When you choose a place to eat through *Le Fooding* you are really choosing what kind of evening to have.

As well as a shift in the style of service and interior design, *bistronomie* ushered in a transformation in the dishes, the ingredients and the culinary canon. Serving a tasting menu means that the choice of recipes and ingredients makes much more sense, and if a customer doesn't like something, well, they'll eat it anyway. Less butter and more olive oil, thanks to a handful of leather-clad wholesalers who bring quality oil from Greece and Sicily. Out with the prestigious pieces of meat and 'superior' fish like sea bass and bream, and in with previously obscure cuts, offal and seasonal fish caught off the Atlantic coast, where two decades of misery for the *petits bateaux* fishermen has been brought to a close by the rise of the neo-bistro. And, most importantly, an incredible variety of vegetables grown just a few kilometres from the city.

Proudly dishing up the 'fifth quarter', as offal is known, and sourcing mud-caked, misshapen vegetables is just another aspect of the open war between two generations and two different classes of bourgeoisie: in recent decades offal had been eliminated from the French bourgeois diet, something that had occurred, consciously or otherwise, as an ideological reaction. These people came from peasant stock and didn't want to be reminded of that fact in what they ate. They felt the need to hide their roots and their past and move towards a brighter future that didn't stink

Above: At Le Comptoir, Nadia
cuts bread while Tommaso cooks.

of manure. This meant being horrified by intestines, and the feeble excuse that some people find it gross got bandied about far too often. *Bistronomie*, along with many other culinary movements across Europe, marks the triumphant return of vegetables and less-desirable cuts of meat to even the most sought-after tables.

A new, younger bourgeoisie has arrived in the guise of the hipsters, the *bobos*, a generation that has not come directly from the farm and has no memory of peasant life and is thus rediscovering and laying claim to it anew. The only three-starred chef recognised as a master by *Le Fooding* is Alain Passard, who, after making a name for himself as *the* point of reference for the secular French art of grilling meat, decided

to take meat off the menu and work solely with plants, soon starting to grow his own. Bertrand Grébaut of Septime, Iñaki Aizpitarte and Giovanni Passerini have all done their time under Passard in the kitchen of L'Arpège.

*

Partly thanks to its irresistible new bistros, the city of Paris then goes through a process of change. This process has a name, and that name is gentrification.

Some chefs and restaurants battle to keep the neo-bistro flame alive as a dishevelled cultural alternative. The working-class and multicultural heart of the neighbourhoods between Belleville, Ménilmontant and Oberkampf has been mortally wounded by the hike in rents and the gradual disappearance of the area's shops, but it is resisting in its own way.

In the final months of 2015 I find myself working in a tiny, vaguely Italian bistro. I'm getting ready to take over and finally

THE PASSENGER   Tommaso Melilli

Pages 74–5: Dinner on a summer's evening at Le Baratin.
Above: The chef at Le Baratin, Raquel Carena, talks to a waiter.
Below: The chefs plan what to do with the day's fresh produce.

THE PASSENGER   Tommaso Melilli

become head chef. I find an apron that looks a lot like those navy-blue ones I used to love so much, and in the lead-up to the big day I start to build relationships with people in the neighbourhood. I select the market stalls from which I want to buy my produce; I make friends with a couple of slightly bewildered spice merchants; I pull off a pretty good deal with a large Middle Eastern grocer's, convincing them to order for me orange-blossom water and organic molasses produced by a Lebanese company I like. They call me 'chef' and quickly start offering me dizzying discounts, and I start to notice a kind of Mediterranean solidarity emerge in our ways of doing business and striking deals. I am quite aware at this time that my reasons for working with the neighbourhood are pretty simple: I don't feel capable of setting up a restaurant and have no idea where to begin. I decide to start by going out on to the street. The result is that the set-up is slow and bumpy, but the merchants are getting to know me and seem to understand that although I've just arrived I want to learn the language and rules of the *tiécar*, which, in the Parisian slang that cuts words down the middle and inverts the two halves, means *quartier*: neighbourhood.

And so I manage to avoid being seen as yet another foreigner landed there just to make some money, and while there are a couple of occasions in the early days when I find my moped has been knocked over, I am swiftly made to understand that if I have any problems they've got my back.

*

And then, on the evening of 13 November of that same year, the whole of Paris finds out that no one has its back. Particularly us, in *our* neighbourhoods, because La Belle Équipe, one of the bistros hit by the gunshots of the Bataclan attacks, is two hundred metres from the restaurant in which I am working. As all hell breaks loose outside, I am frying Milanese cutlets in a pool of hot butter, totally oblivious.

The next day, having gone home at four in the morning in a state of collective shock, we decide to open the restaurant. Nobody comes in to eat, but we make coffee for one or two regulars, incapable of exchanging any words. I am twenty-five and my colleague twenty-three, and we have no idea why we are there. Only afterwards do we begin to understand. We were there that day to send a message that united we resist.

There has been much debate about the neighbourhoods hit by the 13 November attacks, and it is not my place to offer a solution; all there is to say is that the areas of the city wounded that night were those where, albeit with great difficulty, cultural, ethnic and social mixing had been working. They didn't open fire outside Alain Ducasse's restaurants, they did so outside the bistros between Belleville and Goncourt. A bullet went through the window of Septime, which didn't even have a sign outside, yet it was rare to meet anyone who hadn't eaten there at least once.

In the days that followed, *Le Fooding* launched the short-lived movement #tousenterrasse to spread the message against fear and proclaim that we would return to sit outside our favourite restaurants to eat good food, drink wine to celebrate or unwind and sip coffee to sober up or revive.

The city, although suffering, quickly found its feet again – but in some places the wounds haven't healed completely and the scars continue to burn.

*

I've found my notes from an interview I did with Alexandre Cammas in 2015, just a

Along with restaurants, Paris can also lay claim to the first movement that transformed gastronomy into a cultural, social and intellectual event. It was the beginning of the 1970s, and everything that happened in France had to be *new*: *nouveau roman*, *nouvelle vague* and, of course, nouvelle cuisine. Up to that time great French cuisine had consisted of the obsessive reproduction of a set of classic recipes executed to perfection. The emergence of nouvelle cuisine was a reaction to this gastronomic classicism and another application of the dogma of originality subscribed to by all the other arts. And at the heart of this movement, too, there is a guide that acts as a counterbalance to the *Michelin Guide*. In 1973 Henri Gault and Christian Millau published a list of ten commandments that it might be worth reminding ourselves of: 'thou shalt not overcook', 'thou shalt use fresh, quality products', 'thou shalt lighten thy menu', 'thou shalt not be systematically modernist' (this going so far as to contradict Baudelaire), 'thou shalt nevertheless seek out what the new techniques can bring thee', 'thou shalt avoid pickles, cured game meats, fermented foods, etc.', 'thou shalt eliminate rich sauces', 'thou shalt not ignore dietetics', 'thou shalt not doctor up thy presentations', 'thou shalt be inventive'. They would later put their names to a guide that remains hugely influential today. You could credit nouvelle cuisine with championing the concept of produce-led cooking and later the slow-food movement. The likes of the Italian food-hall chain Eataly and even *bistronomie* would not have been possible without those very critics and great revolutionary chefs (such as Bocuse, Senderens and the Troisgros family) who, in their turn, became guardians of the temple. (TM)

few days after the attacks. He didn't want to talk about terrorism and is no longer so willing to talk to me at all. But this was the gist: 'I would like to make one thing clear: *Le Fooding* is not a trend, it's not a fashion, it's not a movement. It's a brand, comprising a paper guide, a website and an app.' He had just sued a well-known frozen-foods multi-national for launching a line of products called Le Fooding. As far as I understand, he won. Cammas, despite talking at length about his grand vision of a multi-ethnic, free, cultural revolution, was actually demonstrating, very clearly, one thing: *Le Fooding* is not everyone's, it's his. And when something is fully yours, it is your prerogative to sell it to the highest bidder.

And that's exactly what he did.

In September 2017 a merger between *Le Fooding* and a big publishing group was announced. A merger that would enable the small, independent and somewhat untamed guide to conquer the world outside France, something that Cammas, despite several attempts, had never quite managed to do. And who do you think it was that became the co-proprietor of the guide that was such an icon for us young chefs? I'll give you a clue: it is associated with a chubby little mascot made of car tyres.

Two months later the *Michelin Guide*, which had always contemptuously ignored *Le Fooding*'s award-winning bistros, bestowed, as if by magic, a first star to *all* of the sixteen neo-bistros crowned by *Le Fooding* in its sixteen unfettered years of existence. We then started to see private events popping up, 'Michelin vs. *Le Fooding*', ticketed at astronomical prices, where one chef with a tall hat and starched white jacket would go up against another with stubble on his chin, a Radiohead T-shirt and that blue apron I had so yearned for. The war was over, and there was now a theme park on the battleground.

It is a pattern we see repeated over and over again in culture as well as in politics: you start a revolution, you get rid of the old people in power with your vision for a new and better world, you eventually get to take their place at the top and then, after twenty years or so, you realise you've become just like them. Maybe your conscience whispers something in your ear every so often, but it's just *so* comfy up there, wouldn't it be a shame to give it all up?

*

Meanwhile, like all successful trends, after fifteen years the concept of *bistronomie* gradually starts to be watered down. Small restaurants and bistros sprout up all over the place like wild garlic in spring. Customers abound, and they're almost always full. Many don't last long, but something new will always appear in their place. There are mumblings among the chefs who enjoyed the golden years that the bubble's about to burst. But that isn't reflected on the balance sheet, and many of them, tired of pulling the shutters up and down by hand every morning and night, open bigger and more comfortable restaurants. The young, bright-eyed chefs opening the new bistros didn't experience the period of conflict with the starred restaurants and so happily move from one to the next, barely noticing the difference. On the plate, the desperate vitality of the *brut* produce, achingly seasonal and served almost in its original form, is starting to wear a little thin. Prices are going up and the produce is getting samey. If you went out for dinner to three different places in the same week you'd risk finding *the same* pigeon, *the same* bonito or *the same* unusual root vegetable with a hint of hazelnut. To be honest, you'd probably find this if you went three times in three different weeks. The fleeting charm of spontaneously composing a dish

has become a mechanical assemblage of three elements, almost at random, sometimes not even considering whether one element goes with the other two. To put it in stylistic terms, pure, elegant minimalism has decayed into something snobby, unnatural and ungenerous; and, in more commercial terms, the chaotic irreverence that was once seductive is beginning to look more and more like a piss-take. What's worse, some of the great chefs of *bistronomie*, after years of sheep's brains and forgotten vegetables, suddenly find themselves serving up caviar, truffle and foie gras, which, although presented with a contemporary flourish, is, after all, exactly what the maestros served in the grand hotels.

The purest chefs and restaurants, the ones who started the movement and have never changed their philosophy, start to show signs of frustration and ennui. Many leave Paris to open places in the countryside or to return to their countries of origin. Some change direction and open new restaurants, and many, almost like ghosts, choose to stay put.

It's always hard to differentiate between History (with a capital H) and the stories of our lives, which makes it difficult to say whether it's the city that's degenerating or just us getting older. *Bistronomie*'s soldiers of fortune are certainly no longer in their twenties, and the restaurant trade demands a certain vigour of leg, knee and liver.

But there's somebody else, someone who's not aged too well, and they're not in the kitchen or behind the counter but sitting at the table. The customers were also in their early twenties back in 2000 and living in apartments (at the very least) in Belleville or Rue Saint-Maur, bought with Mummy and Daddy's savings (when that was still possible). They worked hard and earned well, spending half their money in those bars where the atmosphere was so familiar that they could talk to the waiter like an old friend. Then they moved into their thirties and often stayed after closing time, just for a nightcap, and the nights felt like they'd last for ever. Now they're forty or fifty and still living there, but they're no longer out late, and when someone starts dancing in the bar downstairs they call the police for no other reason than that life is noisy.

*

For the French – well, for Parisians – eating out is not a privilege, it is a right, regardless of their age, class or income. The price matters, of course, but it's not *all* that matters. Every little detail of a bar or restaurant is important and part of a story: most people may not be aware of this or wouldn't be able to explain it, but subconsciously we each see what we want to see. It doesn't matter if it's a kebab shop, a bistro or a Michelin-starred restaurant, whether the interior design is refined, tacky or downright awful. A person either feels comfortable in a place or they don't, and it doesn't take long to find out.

A couple of years ago I had a small dispute with a customer who complained about the price of draught beer in our bar in Gambetta. He explained, seemingly with a bitter taste in his mouth, that he preferred to drink his beer in the dingy bar next door because our neo-bistro wasn't a bar *of the people*. So I went for a beer in the bar next door and was baffled to find that their beer cost sixty cents *more* than ours. This customer was talking about the price, but the price had nothing to do with it. The real problem was our antique tiles and flowery wallpaper, my hipster moustache and wonky vegetables, our natural wines with labels that looked like skateboards, the up-lighting and candles that stood on our tables. The real problem was what we represented.

I left Paris in 2018 and went back to Italy, for a number reasons that I don't need to go into here. Of course, I thought long and hard about it first. During the months of lockdown back in Italy I spent a lot of time contemplating my years in Paris, and as soon as the restaurants reopened I decided to go back and work the summer season in the kitchen of the old place on the hill behind Père Lachaise Cemetery.

Just before her re-election, the mayor of Paris, Anne Hidalgo, approved an exceptional measure to sustain the city's bar-and-restaurant sector at least for the summer. Getting authorisation for outdoor seating in Paris, as elsewhere, used to be a black hole of bureaucracy. The mayor, with this significant announcement, liberalised the use of public space until the end of September: all you had to do was apply on the website and get the form stamped to be able to use pretty much all the room you wanted, including parking spaces. More than twenty very charming streets were now closed off to traffic, enabling the bars and restaurants to make use of them, with the stated objective of transforming the city into one big 'open-air restaurant'. The message was clear: this summer we're not interested in your cars; the priority is to sit around a table at the required distance from one another, to eat and to have a glass or two of wine. Cars aren't part of our city's heritage but restaurants are.

As I finish this piece I'm putting the order in for tomorrow's menu, which is still undecided; it'll come to me at the last minute. In the mornings, when I go to the restaurant to see whether the fish has arrived, I often discover that an anonymous neighbour has knocked over the vase of flowers that we put across the two parking spaces we now have the right to occupy.

We can pretty much put as many tables as we want outside, provided they're

There is only one dish that can *truly* be called a Parisian delicacy, and that is *tête de veau*, boiled calf's head. It isn't readily found these days, but on one day each year, 21 January, when it's absolutely freezing outside, it makes an appearance on the menus of many popular bistros. Calf's head is served on that date in remembrance of the beheading of Citizen Louis Capet, the name given to Louis XVI after France was declared a republic. Some say that it was originally made from pig's head (Louis was known as *roi cochon*, the pig king) but – for reasons unknown – at some point the pig became a calf. Obviously, eating the head of a large animal was a nod to the guillotine, but that wasn't all: the head is a cut of offal which, by definition, was relegated to the plates of peasants and not to be found on the plates of the aristocracy. Making it the delicacy of Paris recalls the French peasants who invaded and conquered the capital with their barricades and pots full of boiled innards. Jacques Chirac, the last truly popular French president, was notorious for his love of *tête de veau*. His appearances at the annual agriculture show – where he would pet an enormous cow – are legendary, and after he said that he enjoyed eating calf's head it would be served almost everywhere he went. It was likely a political move on his part, and he probably grumbled in private that he really couldn't eat another mouthful, but, credit where credit's due, in public he carried on loving it to the end. (TM)

appropriately distanced; the only rule is that we have to start bringing them in at 10 p.m. At that hour in Paris in summer there is still a hint of daylight, as the sun sets very late, and I like it that way. For the first few weeks our no-longer-so-young neighbours, perhaps forgetting that they had once been like us, would call the police because we were working twice as hard right beneath their windows to learn how to adhere to the new rules and maintain the requisite social distancing. But the calls soon stopped, because when the police arrived they saw that we were all on our best behaviour and folding the chairs – and it was only 9.45 p.m. And if there was still a customer or two sitting there, the officers smiled and said we had a little time if we wanted to offer them a cup of coffee or one last glass of wine. 🦅

Le Servan

32 Rue Saint-Maur, 11th arrondissement

An elegant and refined French bistro
with a pronounced Asian – specifically
Filipino – twist. Chef Tatiana Levha is the
wife of Bertrand Grébaut of Septime, the
hottest chef in Paris, but in my opinion she
is better and her plates more generous.
The lunch menu comes in at around
€30 ($35) a head, and in the evening
dishes are between €20–35 ($25–40)
depending on the meat, but the portions are
substantial. Breakfasts are also served.

Aux Deux Amis

45 Rue Oberkampf, 11th arrondissement

This is the perfect example of a
neighbourhood local transformed into a
trattoria and frequented by those in the
know. The patron, David Loyola, moves
between the tables with a handwritten
menu in his order book and slices up a
variety of Iberian cured meats behind the
counter. On Friday lunchtimes they serve
the best steak tartare in Paris, a particularly
rare version because it's horse meat.

Le Baratin

3 Rue Jouye-Rouve, 20th arrondissement

A legendary establishment run by a couple of veterans, both of whom are in their seventies: Pinuche, the sommelier, in my opinion the best host in France (he's also pretty cantankerous, but tell him so, and he'll grunt at you – deep down he likes it), and his wife Raquel, who occasionally still smokes in the kitchen. Exploring their wine list is always an adventure, and their food – traditional cuisine, unfussy but entirely authentic – features some legendary dishes (one must-try evening offering is the veal brain simply blanched with lemon butter and eaten with a spoon).

Bistrot Paul Bert

18 Rue Paul Bert, 11th arrondissement

The menu here features old-school 'meat-and-gravy' cooking – but rarely are such dishes so well executed. Perhaps a little conservative in their wine cellar (if you ask them for a pét-nat they'll give you an earful), but what they do serve is very good all the same – and the excellent and gigantic puddings really are something.

Le Verre Volé

67 Rue de Lancry, 10th arrondissement

This is the place where the very concept of the *cave à manger* was born some twenty years ago, and today it operates as a full restaurant and secret off-duty oasis for other restaurateurs. The generous plates offer an often perfect balance of freshness and well-managed exoticism, bursting with colour, and everything rests on a solid base of juicy meat, butter and mashed potato. There's a wide selection of starters, two dishes of the day at €25 ($30) plus three regular favourites accompanied by potatoes and salad at around €17 ($20). Always open for lunch and dinner, it is loud and downright chaotic – like life itself. (TM)

After decades of being identified with the image of a wealthy, white, heterosexual Parisienne, the image of the French woman has become one of the country's leading exports. Yet on the streets of the capital such women are rarely, if ever, to be found.

THE
PARIS

Sequins in the smoking room of a Paris night club.

ALICE PFEIFFER
Translated by Jennifer Higgins

IENNE

85

Catherine Deneuve, Carla Bruni, Charlotte Gainsbourg ... the list is long and yet so very narrow. France is one of the few countries that presents to the wider world only one iconic representation of its womanhood: the Parisienne.

One feminine identity to symbolise a whole country. She is a Marianne, a personification of the French Republic, a figure of centralised otherness and of national pride. Her relative liberation and her objectification go hand in hand; in 'the most beautiful city in the world' both her insouciance and her vital statistics are essential elements of the postcard image of Paris, a package that also includes the Café de Flore, the Eiffel Tower and the Pont des Arts. She adds 'extra soul', a dose of emotional capital, to the experience of the city.

The Parisienne is supposed to be a sort of heroine, existing outside all biological, generational and social norms. Time, pregnancies, calories, public transport, the weather, the need to earn money, none of these seems to impact her day-to-day life. Her every move is meant to demonstrate unaffected spontaneity but, in fact, does the opposite. As well as the required grace, this fictional character is overflowing with social, ethnic and heteronormative implications that are taken for granted. Generation after generation, Parisiennes share certain characteristics and fulfil the same implicit but omnipresent style criteria: a particular social class, education, appearance, family background and skin tone. A few examples: the famous high-heeled shoes, just like the wicker shopping-basket and the quirky vintage bike, only lend themselves to travelling short distances around central Paris; the predilection for boyfriend jeans and the habit of 'stealing his shirt', as recommended in fashion magazines, are essentially heterosexual; the *de rigueur* red lipstick is only flattering on pale skin; the 'done-undone' hair excludes curly or frizzy varieties; the vintage Chanel bag, excavated from the back of Granny's wardrobe, suggests wealth extending back across several generations.

Who is she? Who is this woman everyone talks about but no one living in the city has ever met? 'The Parisienne is a mythical beast. Like the unicorn. Nobody has ever seen it, but everybody knows all about it,' wrote Jean-Louis Bory in *Les Parisiennes: Les peintres témoins de leur temps*, seemingly as baffled as I am.

It was in the early 2000s, browsing the duty-free boutiques at the Gare du Nord while I waited for the Eurostar to take me back to London, that I discovered this creature for the first time. In the Yves Saint Laurent perfume section, the bottles proclaimed their elegance: Paris, Paris Je t'Aime, Parisienne, Mon Paris. The same symbols recycled in image after image: a lover here, a Haussmann-style building there. Nina Ricci's Love in Paris promised ringlets as free as the head on which they grew. For Guerlain's La Petite Robe Noire the muse was only a silhouette but was still clearly wearing the high heels and beret evocative of the banks of the Seine. The same was true of makeup. I even found a lipstick called Parisienne. The makeup brand Bouche Rouge Paris was entirely dedicated to the concept. These products were the first signs of a trend that was

ALICE PFEIFFER is a journalist for the *Guardian, Vogue* UK and *i-D*, who writes about fashion with a focus on issues relating to diversity, inclusion and the re-evaluation of stereotypes, particularly with regard to French and Parisian femininity. This article is extracted and adapted from her book *Je ne suis pas parisienne: Éloge de toutes les françaises* (Stock, 2019).

'The Parisienne follows trends closely but is wary of them, preferring to wait for them to be validated by luxury brands before she waters them down and makes them more bourgeois.'

soon to spread throughout the industry and its advertising: *French-girl beauty*, a relationship with makeup that was supposedly uniquely Parisian. Lancôme launched special kits dedicated, as its site explained, to Parisienne-style makeup, more carefully cultivated and less casual than it would like to appear.

As time passes and fashions move on, *La Frenchie* evolves without ever really changing because, as I eventually understood, the Parisienne possesses a rare gift: she follows trends closely but is wary of them, preferring to wait for them to be validated by luxury brands before she waters them down and makes them more bourgeois. In the 1970s and 1980s British women wore safety pins in their ears in a rejection of wealth and ornament; the Parisienne wasn't against the idea ... just as long as the pins were solid gold and made by Jean-Paul Gaultier. More recently, when sportswear made a comeback on the catwalk, the Parisienne didn't turn her nose up at big trainers, but she wore them box-fresh, like smart shoes, and got them from Lanvin. Jogging bottoms? Fine, but redesigned by Gucci in 100 per cent silk and worn with a blouse. Paradoxically, she displays both her awareness of the codes and her rejection of their meaning, a position that she sees as the ultimate freedom, without asking herself too many questions about the nature of that freedom.

One of the first visual incarnations of this woman goes back to the Exposition Universelle of 1900: it took the form of a six-metre-high statue by Paul Moreau-Vauthier, called simply *La Parisienne*, depicting a woman dressed in a ball gown. In the early 20th century the Parisienne was a working-class figure and not the well-off *bourgeoise* that she is today. The flirtatious *grisette*, or working girl, became a fantasy figure for servicemen on leave during the Great War, and especially for those Americans who chose to stay in Paris after the war to avoid the puritanism and Prohibition that made life on the other side of the Atlantic rather bleak. After the wholesale slaughter of the war there was an increased female presence in the public arena, and women from all walks of life mingled. This led to a simpler fashion, more suitable for an active existence. As if to distance herself from the corseted image of pre-war women, Coco Chanel launched a collection with masculine elements: trousers, pullovers and short hair, inspired by the boyish look of the 1920s. Although these emancipatory ideals of the pioneers of feminism were diluted and made more luxurious, Chanel did draw on the basic forms of their modes of dress. However, these slender lines were best suited to women who could indulge themselves in such chic luxury hobbies as sailing, playing tennis and taking cruises. Thus haute couture shifted our working-class icon up into a higher social class, creating a new bourgeois version. From now on anyone wishing to proclaim themselves to be a Parisienne had to have the means to buy the trappings that were required. Spend a lot to look as though you've spent nothing, that was the new chic. This appearance of

Above and above right: Parisian underground nightlife on a Sunday morning at Club Péripate.

THE PASSENGER   Alice Pfeiffer

penury was to become an essential aspect of today's Parisienne.

During the Second World War there was a push to maintain Paris's status as the fashion capital of the world, with designers competing to produce extravagant and ingenious clothes using non-rationed materials. As the sociologist Carol Mann explained to me on the subject of fashion during the Occupation: 'What made Paris, and especially Parisiennes, stand out, was that they chose to identify themselves with the national prestige of haute couture that reigned supreme after the armistice. Personal style became almost an act of personal resistance.' US and British servicemen arriving in Paris were amazed by the way Parisiennes looked when, particularly for the British, at home austerity was everywhere. The Parisienne had triumphed over disaster. The myth had taken root.

The spectacle of this femininity fascinates the world, but it is no more 'natural' here in Paris than anywhere else. The historian Emmanuelle Retaillaud-Bajac, in her book *La Parisienne*, describes it as charged with a very specific eroticism. A mixture of chic (distinction and distance) and hot (a certain allure, paired with an element of seduction). 'The notion of "chic" has, since the 19th century, been characterised by a form of elegance both in clothes and behaviour, pertaining to a symbolism of distinction that engages appearance and bodily habitus (the way someone walks, their gestures, etc.) ... And that being "hot" implies a type of seduction that is a little bawdy and provocative with a strong undercurrent of eroticism.' In other words, a mixture of coldness and flirtatiousness leading to interaction that is full of games and things left unsaid. This kind of 'catch-me-if-you-can' approach could even be likened to the famous line '*je t'aime, moi non*

plus' of Jane Birkin and Serge Gainsbourg, Parisians *par excellence* ...

Childish but hypersexual, a near-but-far ambiguity, this is the winning formula for the heroines of French cinema: Isabelle Adjani in Jean Becker's *One Deadly Summer*, Ludivine Sagnier in François Ozon's *Swimming Pool* or Marine Vacth in *Young and Beautiful*. They all play unbalanced Lolitas, hypersexualised bourgeois girls. Free yet full of shame, restrained yet emancipated, powerful yet fragile: the Parisienne is strong ... but always less strong than her man.

If we are to believe the imagery in anglophone guidebooks and films, the Parisienne is incapable of sticking to regular office hours. She's got far better things to do, things that are second nature to her, like reading Sartre in parks (Léa Seydoux in *Blue Is the Warmest Colour*), talking about art, dancing naked in huge Haussmann-style apartments (Eva Green in *The Dreamers*) or running through the corridors of the Louvre (Jean Seberg in *Breathless*).

'Reading is so chic; a book is the ideal accessory!' This desire for intellectualised chic is everywhere in the Parisian fashion world. 'So chic' to have a book sticking out of your pocket! I learned this from a fashion blogger who explained to me that she had found a collection of essays on sociology that was 'just the right size' to fit in her trench-coat pocket with the title peeping out the top. She's not the only one. 'My accessory? The latest Goncourt Prize-winner, ideally in the Nouvelle Revue Française edition – I love their covers,' a press officer in haute couture once told me. What was her greatest fear? 'Coming across as brainless or ignorant.'

And soon the idea spread through the vast machinery of the luxury brands. At the end of one Parisian fashion show the designer admitted to me that the inspiration behind

Notre-Dame was still smouldering when François-Henri Pinault, president of the Kering group and son of its founder François, promised €100 million ($117 million) to rebuild the cathedral. One day later Bernard Arnault, head of the LVMH group, offered double that amount. In 2014 Arnault inaugurated the museum of the Fondation Louis Vuitton in Paris, an explicit response to the Pinault Collection, the family's art collection housed in Venice, which will soon have a museum in Paris. While the Kering Foundation works to tackle violence against women, Arnault's group announced during the Covid-19 emergency that it would produce sanitising gel to distribute to hospitals for free. The media war between the two families – who have also both had issues with the tax authorities – underlines the importance of the luxury sector in France. The LVMH group (standing for Louis Vuitton Moët Hennessy) also controls brands like Christian Dior, Bulgari and Veuve Clicquot as well as hotels, jewellery and watch-making. It boasts France's highest stock-market capitalisation, while Arnault, known as the 'wolf in cashmere', is France's richest man and third richest in the world in 2020. François Pinault, the 'timber merchant', built his empire in the retail sector and began buying up luxury brands in the 2000s, including Gucci and Yves Saint Laurent, generating a turnover of around a third of his rival. But let us not forget the other players in the sector – such as Hermès, which has always been in Arnault's sights – that together account for a quarter of the global market and directly employ 170,000 people in France.

the collection was 'Existential raver – but chic'. The result? A new marketing concept: removing the guilt from the act of buying by lending it an intellectual justification. You assure the customer that they will be both feminine and feminist; on point, engaged but not losing the ability to pull the male gaze. That is why over the years intellectual prowess has been highly prized in the world of advertising: Leïla Slimani, author and Goncourt Prize-winner, makes feminist podcasts for Chanel; Adrien Barrot, a graduate of the prestigious Parisian École Normale Supérieure, is a creative and visual advisor for Hermès; Sophie Chassat, a philosophy graduate from the same university, is a consultant for the luxury group Kering, where she teaches brands to link the ideas of Nietzsche or Spinoza to their commercial vision.

The US perception of the Parisienne only retains its more pleasant aspects (intellectual, passionate, nourished on love and brioche) without delving into the question of the reality of modern France. That isn't what interests Americans. What they want, above all, is to uncover the secret of this being who is the polar opposite of the active New York woman: no Colgate smile, no blow-dried hair, no sneakers hidden in her handbag to put on when she leaves work. No, the Parisienne rejects all the great American myths of success, self-improvement and progression. She is simultaneously a throwback to an old world and the promise of a more balanced future.

The anglophone world has played a key role in maintaining this fantasy. For Woody Allen, Léa Seydoux became Gabrielle in *Midnight in Paris*, a two-dimensional girl whose life consists of walking through Montmartre in the rain; for Tim Burton, Xavier Dolan and Christopher Nolan, Marion Cotillard embodies the woman who is always gentle and elegant, powerful

'The Parisienne rejects all the great American myths of success, self-improvement and progression. She is simultaneously a throwback to an old world and the promise of a more balanced future.'

but restrained; the same is true of Sophie Marceau, Mélanie Laurent and Mélanie Thierry, prized precisely because they never stray from expectations.

Cosmopolitan but never inclusive, the myth of the Parisienne has stuck: a woman superior to others in every way, an object of fascination for the press and cultural commentators the world over. Is it really so surprising? In her 2005 book *French Women Don't Get Fat*, author Mireille Giuliano states that French women (by implication, Parisiennes) 'have better things to do with their time [than working], like waxing their legs and seducing other people's husbands', but she is also a perfect mother, unfailingly patient and flanked by well-brought-up children. Which woman doesn't dream of becoming 'sexy, sophisticated, flirtatious and glamorous', wonders Helena Frith Powell in *All You Need to Be Impossibly French: A Witty Investigation into the Lives, Lusts and Little Secrets of French Women*.

This vision of the Parisienne was soon taken up by advertising campaigns, as luxury brands began to form groups based in Paris. There is LVMH, founded in 1987, which now includes Louis Vuitton, Céline, Dior, Givenchy and Moynat, and there is Kering, with Yves Saint Laurent, Balenciaga, Gucci and Boucheron. Like the Capulets and the Montagues, Bernard Arnault and François Pinault (the directors of LVMH and Kering respectively) competed to restore the image of Paris as an alluring backdrop and an additional, intangible boost to the brand. Paris, the economy of which relies in large part on tourism and luxury, thus needed to be made to fit the image that foreign customers expected, and our female mascot helped to reinforce her own cliché. Everybody had their part to play.

The legend seems to have stood the test of time, given that in May 2018 H&M unveiled a new capsule collection called Bonjour Paris with – predictably enough – Breton tops, polka-dot skirts and other riffs on the *nouvelle vague* theme. A year earlier the journalist Lauren Bastide and the blogger Jeanne Damas created the book *In Paris*, a series of portraits, tips and destinations all with impeccable credentials. Jeanne Damas has made her Parisian life into a whole career: a clothing line, a lipstick and an Instagram account that ticks all the boxes of this fantasy. In order to avoid any impressions that might diverge from this, it is important that tourists arriving in the middle of the working-class area around the Gare du Nord or landing at Charles de Gaulle Airport in the run-down suburb of Roissy shouldn't be disappointed. This first contact with Parisian elegance comes as a surprise to many of them, as it displays a social and ethnic diversity that nobody had warned them about. Many wealthy travellers are so shocked by this that to avoid repeating such a traumatic experience they choose in future to arrive at Le Bourget Airport, which is much neater and tidier.

My aim here, though, is not to attack the stereotype but rather to add into the mix all the other French women, those whose social classes, career choices, religions and skin colours have been sidelined, stigmatised and discriminated against; those who have not been listened to, who have quite simply been prevented from declaring themselves Parisian or French, which they have every right to do. Women from Marseilles, Lyons, Reims or Malakoff, anyone who has an accent: they're beyond the pale. In order to escape from their undesirable suburb they need not only to make a superhuman effort but also to conform unfailingly to the authorised bourgeois stereotypes. Their trajectory must be smooth and imperceptible. Where Britain would applaud a 'go-getter', a 'working-class hero' or a feisty 'self-made woman', Paris sees an 'upstart', a 'careerist' or a 'nouveau riche'. Classism is rarely acknowledged but still fundamental to the construction of this so-called elegance and to any accession to it.

It would be impossible to identify the Parisienne without applying some inter-sectional thinking. Would this imaginary woman shine so brightly without her many foils, all just as feminine as she is, who are hidden in the wings, who fall through the cracks, who are barred from official discourse? 'It is very difficult to define who a Parisienne is. It is, however, easy to identify a woman who is not Parisienne,' wrote Léon-Paul Fargue, as early as 1939, in *Le Piéton de Paris*.

THE CAGOLE

At the other end of the country, around Nice, Cannes and Marseilles, there is the *cagole*, the opposite of the Parisienne but also a far cry from the bombshell cut-out of the French Riviera, a fantasy embodied in the young Brigitte Bardot. Defined as a 'young, extrovert woman, slightly brain-less and vulgar', the *cagole* is constructed not around cosmopolitan femininity but around a beach-sculpted body. She seeks hyper-visibility through her outfits and her waterproof makeup, useful when she cries but also when she's dripping with sweat after a bout of wild dancing.

But fashion loves to hate and hates to love. It will only deign to be fascinated by a blurring of codes if it is done tastefully by a designer and with a firm cultural basis. The women of Marseilles represent a liberty that is impossible in Paris. The *cagole* is always *too much*: 'Too blonde or too brunette or too made up, multi-coloured, bejewelled right to her very fingertips, too much cleavage, too tanned, loud mouthed, tattooed, off her face ... The *cagole* is the epitome of the woman who reminds others that too much is never enough,' goes a comment in the documentary *Cagole Forever* directed by Sébastien Haddouk. She represents a surfeit as opposed to the middle way as defined by the Parisienne. There will be no quarter offered to these fans of nail art, imitation Louboutin stilettos and nights out in clubs getting wasted on overly sweet cocktails, no indulgence for these girls eager to copy the luxury codes of the capital, which are, when it comes down to it, a complete fantasy.

THE ROUNDER WOMAN

In France the female body symbolises the motherland, civilisation, national heritage. Thus, in 2016 Manuel Valls (an ex-prime minister), when reassessing Delacroix's painting *Liberty Leading the People*, declared that 'Marianne is bare breasted because she is nourishing the people. She is uncovered because she is free. That's it. That's the Republic.' Free because she is naked, naked because she is slim, slim because she is forever young. It's the same old story: today, as in the past, the French Republic can only be symbolised by a young, heterosexual white woman whose dress size is definitely no larger than a medium.

These days, however, France is putting on weight. Despite its longstanding reputation, according to the independent research firm Xerfi, more than twenty-three million people in France are overweight or obese, a number that has increased over ten years by 81.9 per cent among women and 57.9 per cent among men. Despite awareness of this transformation in France, overweight people pay a high price, especially in the world of work. According to the International Labour Organisation, obese women in France are eight times more discriminated against when it comes to getting a job and men three times more. It also notes that being obese (according to 79 per cent of women and 73 per cent of men) is one of the most detrimental factors (as much as being over the age of fifty-five, being pregnant or having a visible handicap). Conversely, being physically attractive is seen as an advantage by 66 per cent of women and 65 per cent of men. We can certainly deduce that obesity is perceived as evidence of a lack of self-control and therefore a lack of control over one's life in general, signalling an absence of responsibility and professionalism.

Which specifically Parisian battles are fought on the body of the bigger Frenchwoman? Being slim is, of course, at the heart of the myth of the Parisienne. Mireille Guiliano's *French Women Don't Get Fat* was aimed at Anglo-Saxon readers. Page after page she weaves a fiction of 'natural' slimness; it's not a case of dubious eugenics – far from it! – it's just that French women don't get fat. They lead enchanted lives, real bourgeois-bohemian fairy stories in which there is no place for appetite. According to Giuliano, the French woman 'eats with all five senses' at fixed times – of course – but only (very) small portions; and she always smells good. Her

SQUEAL ON YOUR PIG

In France one of the hashtags used by the movement denouncing violence against women and sexual harassment – particularly in the workplace – was #BalanceTonPorc ('squeal on your pig'), launched on Twitter by the journalist Sandra Muller in October 2017. The expression came from an article in *Le Parisien* about the Weinstein affair entitled 'In Cannes, They Called Him the Pig', and after three days it had already amassed tens of thousands of accounts of women's experiences. In 2017 Muller was one of the 'silence breakers', those who encouraged a debate on gender roles, that *Time* magazine nominated as Person of the Year. And yet #MeToo came in for particularly harsh criticism in France, not least in the letter in *Le Monde* in which a hundred women, including Catherine Deneuve, defended the 'freedom to bother' that they saw as indispensable for sexual freedom and against the drift into puritanical feminism and victim culture promoted by the movement. In France only a few dozen of the accusations on Twitter went to court, and in even fewer cases were the perpetrators fired or found guilty. Muller herself used Twitter to report the harassment she suffered, and, unlike most of the women, she discussed it in detail, giving the full name of the TV executive who had made inappropriate advances towards her. In September 2019 a Paris court found the journalist guilty of defamation, ordering her to pay damages of €15,000 ($17,500) and remove the tweets mentioning the man. In January 2020 Muller appealed, but this is just one example of the fact that the outcome of a #MeToo outing can never be taken for granted.

Above: Hélène, twenty-six.

Above: Marie, thirty.

THE PASSENGER   Alice Pfeiffer

whole life is a staged performance, always worth dressing up for. Her lifestyle makes her naturally irresistible. And skeletal, evidently.

Add to that the French pharmaceutical and parapharmaceutical industries, which spread a neo-liberal concept of weight and health and a sort of 'pharmatisation' of living. Hypermarkets sell both junk food and, in the middle of a layout intended to evoke a pharmacy, anti-cellulite cream, low-cal chocolate, diuretics and hunger-suppressant teas, all with the aim of selling our bodies back to us in a slimmer version and offering us a supposed pseudo-medical control over our well-being. Within this logic of personal development, which has its origins in the self-improvement sector, we exorcise what is undesirable and purge the afflicted body of its poisonous extra kilos. And it is *big* business: health is the second largest export sector for France, generating an annual turnover of €25.5 billion ($30.5 billion); slimming products generate €3 billion ($3.6 billion) according to a Xerfi study.

THE BLACK MARIANNE

In late 2013 Leah Chernikoff, digital director for American *Elle*, asked me to carry out an investigation into the election of Flora Coquerel as Miss France. Coquerel is a French model of half-Beninese parentage, and her win was met with huge levels of animosity. While the French press remained largely silent on the matter, the US media temporarily put aside the myth of the Parisienne and waded in to support Coquerel. Opinions were expressed mainly on social media and were unbelievably aggressive: 'Fuck, a n—' and 'I'm not a racist, but shouldn't it be open only to white women?' were just two of the tweets that Leah Chernikoff sent me. My job was to translate and analyse them.

This was the first article I'd done that made me aware of the danger represented by the ideal image of French women created by the fashion industry. Although the 'black is beautiful' movement has existed since the 1960s in the USA, the industry and the very concept of French beauty still seem resistant to any kind of diversity, at least when it comes to the choice of a national face to represent the country throughout the world. Flora Coquerel was elected Miss Orleans then Miss France, and she received hundreds of abusive tweets and messages, leading her father to place an advert in *Le Monde* denouncing France's pervasive racism. In a nation where race is not discussed it is still a factor and is the cause of much discrimination. France is one of the last countries to adapt to the diversity of its own population. Buying French luxury products seems to symbolise belonging to a society that is now vanished, a fantasy – and it also perpetuates an ideal that smacks of both royalism and colonialism. Snow White, 'the fairest of them all', the girl with pale skin and delicate features represents both the norm and the ideal; all others serve only to reinforce the immutable dominance of this kind of beauty.

In 2018 Virgil Abloh, of Ghanaian origin, was appointed artistic director of Louis Vuitton's menswear collection, becoming the second designer, after Olivier Rousteing, creative director of Balmain, of African descent to take on such a role in France, and Chanel has begun to use more diverse models. But the conundrum remains as to how to create lasting change rather than just being part of a well-intentioned trend – and how to avoid another L'Oréal scenario. L'Oréal boasted of being the 'global leader in diversity'; 'Diversity is in our DNA,' they said. In 2017 the group took on two new faces, Munroe

Bergdorf, a transgender black woman, and Amena Khan, a Muslim model who wears a hijab. However, when these two women made certain political opinions public on social media they were fired. The appearance of diversity was one thing but not the individual opinions that go with it. In reality, with the exception of a few young, independent brands fighting for an alternative way of working – such as Noir/Noir, Nïuku, Proêmes de Paris, Koché and Neith Nyer – these changes are not much more than a way of making money out of being seen to do the right thing.

THE BEURETTE

The words *beurette* and *beur*, which bring an orientalist aesthetic to the Parisian environment, apply to young people of North African descent born in France to immigrant parents. These words are intended to capture a meeting of the supposedly 'retrograde' culture from which these people come and the modernity in which they are growing up. They are reminders of their interloper status, neither French nor Arab. The word *beur* itself comes from the word *arabe* – the two syllables inverted using the common French slang technique of *verlan* – and is thus seen to encapsulate a supposed hybrid of old and new. *Beurette* – the feminine form – at first referred to the cliché of the 'sister', the woman as the link between elements of imported North African culture, seen as rural and unsophisticated, and France. These young women from stigmatised backgrounds that are believed to be 'backward' and 'macho', are perceived as having only one way to succeed and grow: they must take the hand that France holds out to them.

Just like the image of the harem with its mythical concubines, the high-rise tower block, terrifying and impenetrable, is portrayed as being full of imprisoned women, veiled and lascivious. The concept of an Orient lost and found is thus constructed. It's precisely this orientalism based in proximity – a concept of the Other that is at once distant but very close by – that defines the semantic slip that occurred in the early 2000s. If orientalism is perceived as 'a Western mode of domination, restriction and authority over the Orient' (as Edward Said posited in *Orientalism*), and the Orient being not a geographical area but a shifting concept of territoriality, the disadvantaged suburbs of French cities become post-colonial sites. With the 9/11 attacks and the wars in Afghanistan and Iraq as a backdrop, the figure of the terrifying Arab man came into focus. In this context of fear, the *beurette* appeared as a pornographic fantasy. She was defined in opposition to the veiled women whose numbers were increasing in France. But the sexualisation of girls from these poor suburbs, free from bourgeois constraints, was held up as proof of the failure of integration and as the consequence of inherent lustfulness.

She became a fantasy encapsulating all kinds of deviance – an 'authentic *beurette*, a guaranteed 93, a slut in a veil', as described by Michel Houellebecq through his character Daniel, a director of porn-film parodies in *The Possibility of an Island* (2005). (The 93 refers to a district of Paris, Seine-Saint-Denis, which is home to a large number of people of North African descent; see the sidebar on page 52.) This is the literal and symbolic continuation of colonial unveiling, the idea of a woman who is submissive but also hungry for sex. It is a fantasy that came out of the closet in 2016 when Pornhub published its annual report and noted that in France the word *beurette* was top of its search list. It's an image often drawn on by macho French hip-hop artists: the rapper El Matador released a song called 'Les Beurettes Aiment' ('Beurettes Love'): 'Fuck you, all of you, my bitch makes me couscous / The *beurette* thinks I'm cute, in her fishnet stockings / We've got what the *beurs* want, all the *beurettes* … / The *beurette*'s Maghrebi but UV makes her orange / Call her "biatch", she won't mind.'

It's no secret that fashion likes to flirt, just for a season, with whatever society happens to be talking about: catwalks were filled with veiled women, fictional harems, next-generation Princess Jasmines, harem trousers and hijab-inspired veils, but that did not mean that those women whose cultures were mined for inspiration could claim to be the intended clientele. All this only reaffirmed Paris's aesthetic and cultural domination in a toe-curling game of dollies.

So, in fashion terms, the *beurette* embodies the fantasy of a woman who is the antithesis of the French woman. The Parisienne, the colonial woman, controls everything that the Arab woman does not control and becomes the ultimate point of reference for the *beurette*. This Other, symbolising submission and failure, is the ultimate counterpoint and validation of the perennially dominant figure of the Parisienne – an eternal figure of emancipation through codes that she alone can master because she wrote them.

THE QUEER

In 2013 same-sex marriage was finally legalised in France during François Hollande's presidency, and it was disheartening to hear the cries of protest from streets full of thousands of furious members of La Manif pour Tous, an anti-gay-marriage group. This conservative movement had a clear message: the slogan 'One dad, one mum, we don't lie to children' and a baby-blue-and-powder-pink colour scheme.

At the same time, one pop musician

DEMONSTRATION FOR 'ALL'

La Manif pour Tous (Demonstration for All) is a collective of associations established at the time of the Marriage for All bill, which was introduced to extend the rights to marry and to adopt to same-sex couples in France. The collective's stated objective was to 'promote the well-being and future of children, adults and the whole of society' and to act 'for present and future generations'. It describes itself as apolitical with no religious affiliation, but its members include Catholic and Protestant family associations as well as the Vita alliance, which opposes abortion and euthanasia. Since same-sex marriage became legal in 2013 La Manif pour Tous has concentrated its energies on the fight against fertility treatment, surrogate motherhood and gender theory. Fertility treatment for all, part of the controversial bioethics bill, was debated by the National Assembly in September 2019, and the group staged noisy protests. The law, which was passed in July 2020, extends fertility treatment, which has been legal in France since 1984 for heterosexual couples, to all women, including those who are single or in same-sex relationships. The group says it is concerned for the future of the children and for the 'genealogical, emotional, genetic and historical void' that will be created. For tax reasons the collective, which is accused of racism, homophobia and exploitation of children for its own ends, became a political party in 2015, and even though it does not stand in elections it does intervene in national politics, for instance when it supported the candidacy of François Fillon in the 2017 presidential elections.

Above and above right: Saturday
night at Le Chinois in Montreuil.

achieved sudden mainstream fame. Dressed in men's clothes, the singer Héloïse Letissier, going by the stage name of Christine and the Queens (aka Chris), became known for an androgyny that evoked David Bowie, Prince and Marlene Dietrich. The words of her songs questioned gender, and when she appeared on stage or television she didn't hold back from describing herself as pansexual, open to all gender identities without differentiation. Her image, her looks and her songs coincided with the arrival of gender studies in French universities, almost two decades behind the anglophone world. More slowly still, these ideas of gender filtered through to the collective subconscious. From then on the artist became the bridge between 'normal' France and under-represented queer groups.

Chris did not shy away from instructing people and deployed her militant language with great skill, becoming the perfect counterpoint to a reactionary French identity that was still in vogue. Thanks to meticulous marketing she gave visibility to groups that tended to be excluded from the classic representations. Her radicalism was elegant enough to be photogenic, but she deconstructed the Parisian ideal through her androgyny, her muscles and her moves. Could Chris be a mutation of the Parisienne, now capable of juggling queer awareness with unrivalled chic, steering clear of the formerly essential heterosexuality?

One thing is certain: she helped to launch a trend around bi, lesbian and gender-fluid women. Campaigns by Yves Saint Laurent, Diesel and Body Shop all began to use glamorous, slightly androgynous images of women kissing one another. There was a spate of coming out among models (some seemingly for publicity, others for more genuine reasons). Images of queer looks and lifestyles became fashionable, unmissable experiences, the most subversive kind of chic.

Paradoxically – and this is where things get more complicated – clothes are also a key historical player in the question of gender norms. As the historian Valerie Steele shows in her 2013 book *A Queer History of Fashion: From the Closet to the Catwalk*, fashion is also a silent expression of feminist and queer history. Coco Chanel, presumed to have been bisexual, rejected the constraints of marriage. As director of her own company, Chanel expressed her need for liberation through sporting men's clothes and wearing her hair short. Colette, Françoise Sagan and Claude Cahun all expressed their liberty by wearing masculine clothes, symbolising increased independence in the public arena. French fashion used codes that had previously been perceived as lesbian to create new kinds of femininity, in private spheres as much as in public and economic ones. Trousers and men's jackets became part of the Parisienne's wardrobe, and she was now seen as more androgynous than her Latin neighbours. Trench coats, Breton tops and men's shoes (along with other typically Parisian 'basics', as defined by the model Inès de la Fressange) are doubtless the heirs of a specific cultural and intellectual history, but that has now been reduced to a series of codes divorced from their original meanings. The result is strangely distant from the liberty that the pioneers of menswear sought to defend, because this masculine codification and reclaiming of queer makes the Parisienne more feminine than ever: she floats around in her artfully unbuttoned boyfriend shirt, emanating innate delicacy and certainly not equality.

The visibility that the LGBTQ+ community acquired when same-sex marriage was legalised has largely turned into

The campaign for the 2020 municipal election in Paris was an unusual one, with the mayoral race contested by two women with different ideas but united by an unspoken and (in the world of politics) uncharacteristic mutual respect. Neither comes from the *grande bourgeoisie* or attended the country's top universities: Rachida Dati's father was a builder, and Anne Hidalgo, who was re-elected mayor, is the daughter of an electrician. The Franco-Spanish mayor is now an old hand at the Hôtel de Ville, where she has been in office since 2001, first as deputy mayor then in the top job. A long-time socialist, she has become a star of the environmental movement with her policies that support cycling and pedestrians, as is confirmed by her role as chair of the C40, a group of global cities committed to fighting climate change. She has been closely involved in the move to pedestrianise the embankments along the Seine, a measure that was unpopular at first, upsetting the residents of the city's outer zones, and was blocked by the administrative court. But Hidalgo did not give in to the opinion polls (in 2018 only 16 per cent of Parisians were happy with her work) and resubmitted the measure on new grounds that could not be challenged. As well as making large areas of the city centre free of cars she wants to replace thousands of parking spaces with trees. School canteens must serve organic food, and she is dreaming of a blanket ban on single-use plastics. She has denounced and fought Airbnb in an attempt to slow down mass tourism and, in Covid-19, seems to have found an ally in opening up the population's eyes to the need to rethink the city.

pink-washing: queerness has been used in a falsely benevolent way to make money. US gender theorist Judith Butler has written about this classic marketing strategy, which aims to graft a positive image on to brands or political parties. Thus Anne Hidalgo, the mayor of Paris, launched a scheme to turn the Marais district into a little gay capital inspired by that of Tel Aviv. The principal aim was clear: to attract an elite gay clientele, DINK (Double Income No Kids) couples, through marketing and targeting LGBTQ+ tourists. According to the Gay European Tourism Association (GETA), the turnover for LGBTQ+ tourism is $65 billion, around 8 per cent of the whole tourist sector. Hidalgo was clear about her aim to make money here, and MasterCard became sponsors of Paris's Gay Pride, allowing people to make card payments from the floats.

MS AVERAGE

So far I've neglected to mention one more Other, one who is less directly under attack than the types of femininity discussed so far but just as fictitious and essential to the shoring up of our notorious Parisienne. This is a woman who dreams – we are told – of being like the Parisienne, who isn't far from her goal – she is told – but who is destined never to achieve it. She is the 'normal' French woman. But who is this creation of statisticians, known by those in marketing as Ms Average, the so-called 'ordinary' female consumer? She for whom all those women's magazines, the consumer society and the entertainment industry have been created, the woman for whom each image is a direct projection of herself, each advertising campaign a direct response to her personal needs? This average woman obviously doesn't exist any more than the very concept of normality. What do we know about her? She is 40.3

Above: Dancing at La Rotonde.

THE PASSENGER   Alice Pfeiffer

> 'On Instagram the hashtag #frenchgirl brings up over 5.3 million almost identical photos. I've even discovered hairdressers who specialise in the messy Parisienne look and courses at the Sorbonne on *parisianité*, dedicated to this fantasy woman.'

years old, got married when she was 28.6 years old, had 1.7 children and will live to the age of 85.4. She is 1.625 metres tall, weighs 62.4 kilos, has a bust measurement of 93.1 cm, wears size-38 (7 US/5 UK) shoes, is right-handed, is Catholic but doesn't attend mass. She sends 1,056 text messages every year, spends 883 hours online, has 130 Facebook friends and 6.2 friends in real life.

The politician Édouard Herriot invented the concept of the 'average French woman' in 1924 with the aim of establishing her statistics. The profile of this average woman is a remix of elements that say more about the time in question than about the woman herself, and the whole thing bypasses any reference to ethnicity, which is illegal in France. In other words, the average French woman has no colour or any diverse characteristics of any kind: above all, she is French. Although her identity is completely artificial she nevertheless plays a key role in supporting the Parisienne's unique identity, acting as her mirror. This shadowy Other belongs neither to the elite nor to the oppressed minorities, instead occupying a poorly defined space and holding up a mirror to the Parisienne, envying her while simultaneously turning her back on oppressed groups. She dreams of being a Parisienne, and the whole capitalist machine assures her that she is just a few steps away from her dream.

The Parisienne is a prism for the aspirations and tensions of her era, so it is no surprise that she changes over time. Today she is ultra-connected and globalised, as befits our time. Whole careers, especially since the arrival of social networks and Instagram, are dedicated to staging these various lives. On Instagram the hashtag #frenchgirl brings up over 5.3 million almost identical photos. I've even discovered hairdressers who specialise in the messy Parisienne look and courses at the Sorbonne on *parisianité*, dedicated to this fantasy woman. Fame, even a tiny amount of it, becomes a fundamental right and a target to which to aspire, a central promise of democratic capitalist society – which nobody really believes in.

However, without Ms Average there would be no Parisienne. Without a girl dreaming of Inès de la Fressange and sporting Chanel bags – who might, if she's lucky, be able to get hold of a high-street copy – the fantasy of the Parisienne and her consumption would collapse. And what would Paris be without the myth of the Parisienne? Gender studies doesn't allow the use of the word normal – it's too politically and culturally loaded, an impossible concept. Nowhere does the norm weigh so heavily as it does in Paris. ✒

This article is an adapted extract from *Je ne suis pas Parisienne: Éloge de toutes les françaises* by Alice Pfeiffer (Stock, 2019).

The Fear
of Letting
Go

Samar
Yazbek

Since childhood the writer Samar Yazbek, originally from Damascus, had dreamed of living in the City of Light, enchanted by the way it was portrayed in art and literature, but when the civil war in Syria forced her to move to Paris, she had to contend not just with the real city as she found it but with the fear of losing contact with her homeland and her native Arabic language.

Translated by Nashwa Gowanlock

I didn't choose Paris to be my place of exile, it came about by chance. And I didn't decide to be exiled from my country, I was forced into it. I'm saying this so that it doesn't appear to readers that, like many other writers, I chose to live in Paris in the pursuit of knowledge and culture in the City of Light and so that I don't begin by talking about the Paris that writers and artists dream of.

The reality is that Paris had occupied my mind since long before 2011, because I am a writer who lives within her pages, books and novels more than in the actual place her feet happen to tread. It was like a delightful labyrinth of locations that inhabited my mind through reading about them. I had lived in the Paris of my imagination – which had been written about by exiles, poets and dreamers and from which philosophers had emerged – more than my lived reality in Damascus. My body was in Damascus, but Paris and other capitals of culture and art resided in my mind. Now I live in Paris, but my mind is in far-off Damascus. This is a new kind of labyrinth, but its alleyways carry the stench of war and death.

When I arrived in Paris in 2011, I thought it was a short stop-off on my way back to Damascus. To put it another way, Damascus represented history and a sense of belonging to the idea of revolution and democratic change that I had dreamed of at the time, and in Paris, until I was awarded French citizenship in 2018, I was a political exile dreaming of returning to Damascus. Back then, in those first years following my arrival, I wasn't thinking of looking for the Paris that had occupied my thoughts since childhood, the Paris in which James Joyce, Ernest Hemingway, Michel Foucault, Pierre Bourdieu and

SAMAR YAZBEK (pictured right) is a Syrian journalist and writer, one of the most high-profile intellectuals in the fight against the regime of Bashar al-Assad. After suffering threats, intimidation and psychological torture, in 2011 she fled Syria, returning clandestinely to document the situation in the war-torn country, an experience that she wrote about in *The Crossing: My Journey to the Shattered Heart of Syria* (translated into English by Nashwa Gowanlock and Ruth Ahmedzai Kemp, Ebury/Rider, 2016). Her work has been translated into numerous languages and has been recognised with many awards, notably the French Best Foreign Book Award, the PEN-Oxfam Novib, PEN Tucholsky and PEN Pinter awards. Her latest book is a novel, *Planet of Clay* (World Editions, 2021).

others had lived. To my mind it felt neutral, shrouded in mystery and darkness; I didn't really see it.

Right from my very first day in Paris the one thing I wasn't able to resist was the way the Parisian night was lit up; it was enchanting. This was more powerful than any feelings of being in a temporary place or of being a refugee and any sense of estrangement which that engendered. I would slip out of my home in pursuit of the city's lights and to embrace the sky at night while walking its pavements and along the banks of the Seine, despite the suffering I felt over the massacre taking place on the other side of the world, where Syrians are dying every day. That was where I had to travel to from time to time in order to write and be active for the sake of the Syrian cause, to sneak across the Syrian–Turkish border and return covertly to my homeland where I would toil in the hope of the dictator's downfall. But the emergence of ISIS, the deaths and kidnappings of friends and the infernal war that followed the revolution in Syria forced me to return to Paris. From that time onwards I knew that this city – whose culture had inspired me from a young age to dream of pursuing a path of literature, creativity and art – was the one in which I would live. This was a number of years ago. Paris has accounted for much of my passion for life, despite my preoccupation with writing fiction, documenting events and working in civil society, because once again this city dominated my mind. I have rediscovered it in several stages, and I rediscovered myself at the same time. Yes, it is the city that offers unconditional freedom, but it wasn't the Paris I had read about. Nevertheless, it was still, for an exiled writer like me, able to enchant.

The first thing I did was search for traces of the books I had read about the city by foreign authors. Where did James Joyce sit? In which parts of the city had he lived? Who would meet in this place or that? Where did Ernest Hemingway, whose life I traced through his book *A Moveable Feast*, write? I searched for echoes of his presence in the Latin Quarter, in the home that he rented and in the cafés he would frequent. I walked in his shoes all over the city and discovered that only a few remained. I tracked the footsteps of Henry Miller from *Quiet Days in Clichy*, his book about Paris. Place de Clichy became a location to which I would return repeatedly and look for the places he visited and wrote about. Looking at them with the eyes of the writer himself as well as with my own, I could see the difference. I hunted for those details that transform reality into imagination and imagination into reality. To me this was more important than reading anthropological and sociological research as a way to understand the changes the city had undergone. Café de Flore and Les Deux Magots were where I hoped to catch glimpses of Simone de Beauvoir, Jean-Paul Sartre and others. Then I stopped, because there were no glimpses to catch.

My plan had been to acquaint myself with Paris from the perspective of those favourite writers of mine who had lived in and written about the city, but the Paris of my imagination was not to be found there. Les Deux Magots was packed with the bourgeoisie, with tourists, a few media personalities and the odd cultural figure. It was in these cafés that I spent my days at first. What I found strange initially but then became accustomed to was how the cleaners were all immigrants and black people – whereas the women with whom I would launch into extended conversations were also mostly Arab, African, South Asian or from the Far East. This is the underbelly of Paris no one wants to talk about. The Paris that – whether we like it or not – separates its citizens from those who have sought refuge there. I was a middle-class political refugee forming an impression of a city through literature, ideas and art, so much so that I spent a great deal of time enquiring about the places that Frida Kahlo and Francis Bacon had visited and where they had lived. I wasn't one of those who had been crushed by Paris, as many are. I would tell myself that this is the way with wars. What had happened to intellectuals during the Second World War after they left Europe had happened to me. But for a woman arriving from the Middle East it was different. Yet I admit that I was and still am – despite these changes – enamoured with the city that was fundamental to the transformation of my psychological, artistic, literary and political consciousness. I can say that, yes, a woman like me can experience the meaning of freedom here, whether or not this city crushes its immigrants and its underprivileged.

Over the course of ten years in Paris I have moved home six times – from the centre out to the north and down to the south. I became familiar with the gritty underside, deep in the heart of Belleville's alleyways; I came to know the city's magical nights and its most elegant streets, Rue Montmartre and Rue Montorgueil. Then something began to weaken my connection to my identity, which had become dulled, as I travelled to several European cities to promote my books. I started to find that, even though Paris remained unique to me, there was something strange happening to all these cities, from London to Berlin, Stockholm, Rome and others; they were becoming less enchanting, acquiring instead cosmopolitan, consumerist characteristics that were transforming them into homogenous markets. The distinctive features and the historic and cultural characteristics of each city quite often disappeared for the sake of a marketable, consumerist identity. You would find the same brands and Chinese products in any one of these cities' underprivileged neighbourhoods as you would in all the others. This also generally applies to the wealthier parts of town, as though the entire world is moving towards becoming one large market. Despite the fact that architecturally Paris is like an open-air museum, and the fact that the geometric design of the city is so remarkable, shaped as it is like a spiral with a series of overlapping circles, ultimately this will all melt away, morphing instead into a new way of living that is savage and consumerist. The image of us all squashed inside the Paris Métro, huddled underground, running at full speed to our businesses and our work, makes me feel as if I'm at the entrance to a tunnel called the end of the world.

After rediscovering Paris through books and being disappointed in a way that I don't attempt to conceal, despite having expected a city quite unlike the one my beloved authors had written about in

the early/mid-20th century, still the traces of that lustre had faded to a disheartening degree. What had let me down in my rediscovery of Paris was language. It was a new layer in my rediscovery of the city, since a different Paris appeared after I began reading in French. Despite having already read Walter Benjamin in Arabic, I will not forget that when I read his book about the covered arcades of Paris and then visited them once again my sense of the city was revived. This also made a connection with Damascus, especially in the architecture of the old alleyways, which took me back to the markets and lanes of my home city. After that I began to pursue Paris through the eyes of its local writers and through the press and the internet and discovered a lively world, despite the gulf that separates it from the aesthetics of its beautiful past. Yes, language is the key to a wealth of knowledge, and, even though at first I resisted learning French and was protective of my Arabic because – as the poet Mahmoud Darwish put it – my language is me and I am my language and because I feared that if I learned French I would lose the last vestiges of my identity in exile, French became the gateway to a deeper discovery of Paris. I still remember the horror I felt when I read about the Grand Paris project and visualised how the old Paris – which they are attempting to modernise with perpetual projects to renovate its buildings and museums – would drift away and be replaced by skyscrapers or hemmed in by concrete forests. I wondered whether the Grand Paris project that they dream of implementing will erase the lingering traces of the Belle Époque that once established the city as a global beacon of thought, culture and art. But can Paris be reduced to its stones, its buildings and its history? I know that the world has changed, that the glory days where art and culture were a beacon to mankind has passed and we have entered an alarming era of fluidity of meaning, as Zygmunt Bauman said. Despite this, I still say that we are here and we are able to invent meanings and renew them.

After unearthing this new layer of Paris through the French language, I had to live the city as it was, far from the nostalgia of the past and the shedding of its attractive qualities. I decided I would get to know a different side of the city. I planned to visit the theatres and museums, public spaces, the cinema, to visit libraries and to read there and keep track of new books and publications, intellectual and literary debates and the political situation. I was at the heart of the action, but I wasn't part of the city's intellectual society. I didn't try to enter it and preferred to remain on the sidelines, even though my books are published in French translation and, as far as I'm aware, receive their share of readership. My initial disappointment with the obvious contradiction between the Paris of the past and the intellectuals and artists who lived there and what the city has now become made me keep my distance. The paradox was that I was deeply immersed in the discovery of Paris, and the city offers itself graciously to anyone on the hunt for knowledge, art and literature. I was eager to get to know the city and to savour its art. It is true that Paris changed me and helped me gain a great deal of knowledge, especially in the fine arts and theatre. It changed me and, after war had destroyed all that was beautiful within me, it enabled me to go back to a time when discovering a book or a painting would make me feel happy for days on end. Yes, Paris and its art, its lights and its many layers that I had willingly and consciously chosen is what rekindled this excitement for me, without attempting to deceive me about what was taking place on its other, less agreeable face, one that most large and great cities also possess.

Lately, and during the quarantine that followed the Coronavirus pandemic, as residents of Paris we were allowed to walk around the city only for a specific length of time over limited distances, I would go out for a walk wearing a mask for an hour in the morning and an hour in the evening. I saw the museums, the Eiffel Tower and the famous squares with their statues all deserted as if we were awaiting the Day of Judgement. My heart trembled, and I cried because for a moment I realised that I was now in an imprisoned city, that I was a woman who had escaped war and that all this beauty had been left to become a void and a state of nothingness and that my feet were

now treading the asphalt of the city I had dreamed of for so long, yet my mind was elsewhere. My whole life, before the revolution and war, I had hoped one day to live in Paris. Now I do live in Paris, I can feel it and embrace its history and culture, but my mind is not here with me; my mind is in Damascus, not simply because it is where I used to live, not just because it is my home, but because it is the oldest continuously inhabited capital city in human history. Different civilisations and religions have passed through it and it has survived, but today it is being destroyed and is disappearing in the most brutal and barbaric of ways. And now that I am without Damascus I cannot let myself go and fall in love with this city, Paris, which has given me so much and taken so much away from me.

I don't know now if I will enter a new phase of discovery in this multi-faceted and complex place, since the acquisition of knowledge doesn't stop. It is quite usual to rediscover ourselves as our lives progress, but here I feel as though I've been strung up on the gallows. Every day I walk along the Seine, and I think of the river Barada in Damascus drying up through drought. I visit the theatres of Paris, and I think of our war-ravaged theatres. I am afraid of taking the plunge and allowing myself to love this city in case I lose my memory completely and forget who I am and how to write in my own Arabic language. When it comes to the beauty of this city, I experience a terrifying split personality. I know that there is some flaw that doesn't allow me to be capable of belonging to it – maybe it's too early to talk of this and maybe I am simply a writer who has not been able to get over the suffering of war and exile. What I do know is that on the last day of quarantine I went for a walk at high noon. The sun was scorching in Rue du Commerce in the 15th arrondissement, the street was empty, and I suddenly spotted a mirage in the distance and smelled the scent of noon in Damascus. At that moment I knew that Paris had started to become a genuine part of me, and this made me quake with fear. At that moment I was fading away and losing a bit of myself. I was touching a severed body part, and that body part was my head. ✒

How the Murders of Two Elderly Jewish Women Shook France

The violent deaths of Lucie Attal and Mireille Knoll within a year of one another, and the controversies surrounding the subsequent investigations, fanned the flames of the debate on religion in France. Were the murders motivated by antisemitism, and is the country witnessing the growth of a new form of Islamic antisemitism, exploited by right-wing politicians and intellectuals to stir up Islamophobia?

JAMES MCAULEY

Left: The entrance to a synagogue in Belleville.

The body landed in the courtyard not far from the building's bins. Shortly before 5 a.m. on 4 April 2017 a 65-year-old woman was hurled from the third-floor balcony of a social-housing project in the 11th arrondissement of Paris, a rapidly gentrifying area on the eastern side of the French capital. An hour earlier that same woman – a retired doctor and kindergarten teacher – had been asleep in the small apartment where she had lived for the past thirty years. When she woke up she saw the face of her 27-year-old neighbour in the darkness. The man, who still lived with his family on the building's second floor, had first stormed into another apartment, whose tenants had locked themselves in a bedroom and called the police. By the time he had climbed up the fire escape into his victim's apartment, three officers were present in the building.

The autopsy would later reveal that the woman's skull had been crushed, most likely with the telephone on her bedside table. Before and after his victim lost consciousness, the assailant beat her until the nightgown she was wearing – white, with a blue floral pattern – was soaked with her blood. He then dragged her body to the balcony of the apartment and threw her over the railing – exactly the same way, he told prosecutors, as John Travolta does in *The Punisher*, the film he had been watching before the attack. 'I killed the *sheitan*!' he yelled from the balcony, according to testimonies given by neighbours. *Sheitan* is an Arabic word for devil. Neighbours heard him repeatedly chant '*Allahu akbar*'.

The victim was Lucie Attal, an Orthodox Jewish woman who sometimes used the name Lucie Attal-Halimi. The perpetrator, who confessed to the crime, was Kobili Traoré, a Franco-Malian Muslim. He later told the authorities he knew that his victim was Jewish. According to her family Attal had long felt afraid of Traoré. Her brother, William Attal, told me that Traoré had verbally abused her in the building's elevator, and she had said she would only feel safe if he were in prison. In fact, Kobili Traoré may never go to prison for the killing: he has been in psychiatric detention since the night of the crime.

In the immediate aftermath of Attal's death there was virtually no public discussion of her killing. With the upcoming presidential election dominating headlines, the defenestration of a Jewish woman in the 11th arrondissement of Paris was treated by the mainstream French press as a *fait divers*, the term used to describe a minor news story, which led to considerable outcry in the Jewish community. But after the victory of Emmanuel Macron the case returned to the forefront, becoming a new frontline in France's culture wars, among the most explosive in Europe.

The French Republic is founded on a strict universalism, which seeks to transcend – or, depending on your viewpoint, efface – particularity in the name of equality among citizens. In a nation that tends to discourage identity politics as *communautaire* and therefore hostile to national cohesion, the state not only frowns on hyphenated identities but does

JAMES MCAULEY is the Paris correspondent for *The Washington Post*. An alumnus of Harvard and Oxford universities, he is an expert on French history. His first book, *The House of Fragile Things* (Yale University Press, 2021), investigates the history of Jewish art collectors in France between 1870 and 1945 and the fates of their art collections that were looted by the Nazis and their French collaborators as their families were sent to the concentration camps.

not even officially recognise race either as a formal category or a lived experience. Since 1978 it has been illegal in France to collect census data on ethnic or religious difference on the grounds that these categories could be manipulated for racist political ends.

But eliminating race did not eliminate racism or racist violence. In the case of Lucie Attal, the inescapable fact of the matter is that a Muslim killed a Jew in a society where those distinctions are supposed to be irrelevant. Long after the fact, exactly how to label Attal's death remains a matter of bitter, and perhaps unresolvable, debate. To examine the case is to examine the fractures of the French Republic, the contradictions in the stories a nation tells itself.

Traoré has vehemently denied that antisemitism played a role in his crime, claiming instead that he acted in the throes of a psychotic episode triggered by cannabis. But for William Attal, the only way to understand his sister's death is as an act of antisemitic violence. 'He knew very clearly that Judaism was the motor of her life, that she had all the external signs of Jewishness,' Attal said. When we met in a café in the Paris suburb of Nogent-sur-Marne he wore an anonymous red baseball cap instead of anything that might identify him as Jewish. 'We have the obligation to cover the head, but we do not have the obligation to wear a kippa,' he said. 'Understand?'

In February 2018, after considerable public outcry from Jewish organisations, who accused the criminal justice system of a cover-up, a French judge added the element of antisemitism to the charges against Traoré. But the case is far from closed. In July 2018 a second court-ordered psychiatric examination declared that the perpetrator was not of sound mind

THE RETURN OF ANTISEMITISM

France reacted with horror to the attack at Chez Jo Goldenberg on 9 August 1982; it was the most serious assault on the Jewish community in Paris since the Second World War. The Jewish restaurant in the Rue des Rosiers was hit first by two grenades then attacked by three terrorists who opened fire, killing six people and wounding twenty-two. Only two months earlier Israel had invaded Lebanon, sparking a war and a string of terrorist atrocities. The day after the massacre President Mitterrand set up an anti-terrorist unit reporting directly to the Élysée, leap-frogging the entire hierarchical structure. The first result was the surprise arrest of three Irish-nationalist militants who had taken refuge in Paris. Weapons and explosives were found in an apartment, but the three men arrested insisted they had never owned them, and in the space of a few months the case against the men, who became known as the 'Irish of Vincennes', collapsed spectacularly. The press then turned its attention to the methods adopted by Mitterrand's unit, and it emerged that the gendarmes had planted the weapons. It took almost four decades for any of those responsible for the attack at Chez Jo Goldenberg to be arrested, the most recent being in Norway in September 2020. It was carried out by the Fatah Revolutionary Council, a Palestinian paramilitary movement founded by Abu Nidal, a controversial, murderous figure suspected of collaboration with the Israeli intelligence agency Mossad. In 2019 the former head of the French domestic secret service (DST), Yves Bonnet, revealed the existence of an agreement with the terrorists under which they would promise to end attacks on French soil in exchange for immunity.

and was unfit to stand trial, a conclusion that was also reached by a court of appeal in December 2019. If he cannot be held accountable for his actions, Traoré cannot, legally speaking, be said to have had a motive. There is the possibility that Attal will have officially died in a random act of violence, as if she had simply been in the wrong place at the wrong time. [In April 2021 France's highest court, the Cour de Cassation, upheld the ruling that Traoré was suffering a psychotic episode at the time of the murder, while reconfirming the antisemitic nature of the crime. Demonstrations were organised in the wake of the ruling, and the victim's sister has stated she will now bring a separate legal case in Israel.]

During the months of confusion, indecision and silence that followed the killing, people from every side of France's political debate seized upon the case as evidence of whatever position they already held. In time, the story of Lucie Attal would become the inspiration for any number of politicised narratives, hardly any of which took into account the woman who had died or even her actual name.

*

On 10 April 2018 – one week after the killing and three weeks before the presidential election's first round – Marine Le Pen sat down for an interview with the newspaper *Le Figaro*. Two days earlier Le Pen had shocked much of the country by claiming that the Vichy government's participation in the Holocaust 'was not France' and insisting that France was 'not responsible' for the so-called Vel d'Hiv round-up of Parisian Jews in 1942. It was time, she said, for the French to be 'proud to be French again'.

The Vel d'Hiv round-up ranks among the darkest days in modern French history and is known even to schoolchildren as a synonym for national shame. On 16 July 1942 approximately thirteen thousand Jews were arrested and detained in the now-demolished Vélodrome d'Hiver racing arena in the shadow of the Eiffel Tower. From there they were deported to Nazi concentration camps. Few of the deportees ever returned. What lingers in the public consciousness is this: it was French police officers who carried out this assault on their fellow citizens, not their Nazi occupiers.

Pressing Le Pen on her Vel d'Hiv comments, the journalist from *Le Figaro* asked how she would respond to the condemnations her remarks had elicited from Jewish groups and the state of Israel. For the daughter of a convicted Holocaust denier trying to 'de-demonise' her party, these kinds of questions risked giving Le Pen precisely the kind of publicity she was desperate to avoid. So she changed the subject.

'What I'd rather we talk about is Islamist antisemitism,' Le Pen said. She had an anecdote ready. 'Several days ago a 61-year-old woman was thrown, defenestrated from the third floor, because she was Jewish. She was threatened and called a "dirty Jew" by her neighbour for several days – and that we never talk about.'

During a presidential election campaign that revolved around questions of national identity, Le Pen became the first public figure to discuss the killing of Attal. Yet Le Pen did not mention Attal by name, and she was wrong about her age. During the interview, Le Pen's Twitter account mentioned that the victim – again unnamed – had been seventy. In fact, she had been sixty-five, but the details about the actual woman who had been killed were never the point.

On one level Le Pen's rhetorical pivot to 'Islamist antisemitism' was an attempt to

Above and right:
Details of the buildings
where the two victims,
Mireille Knoll and Lucie
Attal, lived.

'But one reason the case became so notorious is that it fits into what has become a common narrative. France is the only country in Europe where Jews are periodically murdered for being Jewish.'

distance herself from her party's history of Holocaust denial and to court Jewish voters anxious about the rise of Islamist terrorism. But for Le Pen, the killing of Attal – even before any of the details were known – served a much broader purpose. It was perhaps the most emotive example of what had been the National Front's underlying message throughout the campaign and which of late had trickled into the mainstream right: that the French Republic and Islam were fundamentally incompatible.

*

On 10 July 2018 Kobili Traoré was formally interviewed by the judge investigating the case. Three months earlier, on the night of the crime, he had been taken into custody, and police discovered that he already had a considerable criminal record, having served time for aggravated violence and drug dealing. But when police tested him that night the toxicology report showed a high level of cannabis in his bloodstream, and his behaviour was erratic enough that he was immediately sent to a psychiatric hospital. There he was examined by a respected psychiatrist, Daniel Zagury, who concluded that he was not of sound mind and was therefore not in a fit state to be interviewed by prosecutors. In the months that followed Traoré remained in the hospital, under warrant but without being formally charged.

When the investigative judge finally interviewed Traoré in July the young man

insisted that antisemitism had not been his motive. 'I have never had problems with Jews before,' Traoré said. He claimed that the killing had happened during a bout of temporary insanity. On the night of 4 April he had been with a friend, he said, watching *The Punisher*. Before turning on the television the two had gone to evening prayers at the Omar mosque in the Rue Morand, according to an investigative account by the French journalist Noémie Halioua. (Mohammed Hammami, that mosque's former imam, was expelled from France in 2012 when Traoré was a teenager for having allegedly incited hatred in sermons.) Traoré, who by all accounts was not a particularly observant Muslim, told the judge that he and a friend had gone to pray that night because he had not been feeling well. 'I was feeling like I'd been oppressed by an exterior force,' he said in his interview, according to the transcript. 'A demonic force.'

The young man defined that 'demonic force' as a kind of delirium over which he had no control, induced by the several joints he had smoked. (According to *Le Monde*, Traoré smoked between ten and fifteen joints a day.) Asked why he had entered Attal's apartment, he had no answer. 'I still do not know,' he said. 'It could have fallen on anyone – the Diarras, my family,' Traoré claimed, referring to the family whose apartment he had first entered, before climbing up from their balcony to the apartment of the woman he killed. Yet 'it' did not fall on anyone else; it fell on Lucie Attal.

At one point in Traoré's interview with prosecutors he was interrogated about what he had said at the scene of the crime:

INVESTIGATOR: Your family heard, and your sister and your mother have confirmed that you were not feeling well and that you were repeating 'Sheitan, sheitan.' What does that mean?
TRAORÉ: It's the demon in Arabic.
INVESTIGATOR: Do you speak Arabic?
TRAORÉ: No.
INVESTIGATOR: Doesn't it seem bizarre that you would designate [Attal] as the devil in a language you don't speak?

In Zagury's report, seen by Le Monde, the psychiatrist concluded that it was unlikely the killing was a premeditated antisemitic hate crime. However, the psychiatrist saw plenty of antisemitic mechanisms at work, including Traoré's own confessions that he had somehow been triggered by the Torah and the menorah he saw in Attal's apartment.

In his report Zagury pointed out that the particular form delirious episodes take is always shaped by 'society's atmosphere and world events'. 'Today, it is common to observe, during delirious episodes among subjects of the Muslim religion, an anti-semitic theme: the Jew is on the side of evil, the evil one,' he wrote. 'What is normally a prejudice turns into delirious hatred.' This, he concluded, is precisely what happened once Traoré broke into Attal's apartment. 'The fact that she was Jewish immediately demonised her and amplified his delusional experience ... and caused the barbaric surge of which she was the unfortunate victim.'

*

Lucie Attal's apartment block – 30 Rue de Vaucouleurs – is a classic habitation à loyer modéré, or HLM, one of the many social-housing projects developed in this part of Paris in the early 1980s to provide residents, many of them immigrants, with affordable housing in a fairly central location. In recent years the neighbourhood has become the kind of place where trendy cafés, natural-wine bars and experimental restaurants with months-long waiting lists seem to anchor every block.

A squat, angular structure plastered with grimy grey tiles on a short, treeless street, the apartment block is as far as central Paris gets from 19th-century grandeur. But the Rue de Vaucouleurs is hardly an example of the 'social and ethnic territorial apartheid' decried by then prime minister Manuel Valls in January 2015, as he lamented the rise of home-grown Islamist extremism following the Charlie Hebdo attack. It is also a remarkably diverse neighbourhood, which appears at first glance to be a testament to the successes of the French social model of integration, not its failures. Local residents describe a far more complex reality than often appears in public discussions of the killing.

One of Attal's neighbours, Faim Mohamed, told me he had lived in the building since 1997. 'Life was cool,' he said, insisting that the only tensions he has ever felt came after Attal's death, not before. 'Since the murder, everyone is suspicious. They're worried if someone is following them when they enter the building.'

Another man, from Morocco, who declined to give his name, was Attal's neighbour on the third floor. I met him as he was bringing in groceries one afternoon, and his eyes filled with tears when I asked him if he knew the woman who had been killed. 'She was someone who was very good,' he said, adding that she had designated him her Shabbos goy because he would do little household tasks

Below: An elderly woman walks through a market beneath an elevated section of the Paris Métro.

for her on Shabbat that she could not do for herself. He said he had been on vacation when the killing happened, visiting family in Morocco. 'If I were there, I would have intervened. But I was not,' he said. A Muslim himself, he was adamant on one point: 'A Muslim would not do this.'

But one reason the case became so notorious is that it fits into what has become a common narrative. France is the only country in Europe where Jews are periodically murdered for being Jewish. No fewer than twelve Jews have been killed in France in six separate incidents since 2003: Sébastien Selam, Ilan Halimi, Jonathan Sandler, Gabriel Sandler, Aryeh Sandler, Myriam Monsonégo, Yohan Cohen, Philippe Braham, François-Michel Saada, Yoav Hattab, Lucie Attal and Mireille Knoll.

In each of these cases at least one of the perpetrators was from what the French call *minorités visibles*, or visible minorities, which typically refers to those of North African or West African descent, and in most cases the perpetrators have been linked with some form of extremist Islam. In nearly every case the victims have been either identifiably Jewish or personal acquaintances of the perpetrator. Almost all perpetrators and victims have been lower middle class, residing in the same diverse neighbourhoods, the same streets or even the same buildings.

In 2006, for instance, there was the notorious murder of Ilan Halimi, in which the so-called Gang des Barbares – a band of French-born children of Muslim immigrants from West Africa and North Africa – lured the 23-year-old Halimi, who sold mobile phones off the Boulevard Voltaire, on a date with a pretty girl. They had hoped to extract €450,000 ($535,000) in ransom money from Halimi's parents, whom they assumed to be rich because they were Jews. But the Halimis lived in Bagneaux,

the same low-income *banlieue* as the gang members themselves. Ilan Halimi was imprisoned and tortured in the basement of a public-housing project for three weeks. He was found on the train tracks in Sainte-Geneviève-des-Bois, to the south of Paris, his body naked and burned.

For Rachid Benzine, a scholar of Islam and a well-known French public commentator, these killings are best understood in the context of what he calls post-colonial antisemitism. 'For me this is a holdover from the colonisation of Algeria, linked to the treatment of Algerian Jews compared with Muslim natives,' he said. In 1870, for instance, the so-called Crémieux decree secured full French citizenship for all Jewish subjects residing in Algeria, whereas Arab Muslims remained under the infamous *code de l'indigénat*, which stipulated an inferior legal status, essentially until 1962. The legal disparity continued even after Algeria won independence, when hundreds of thousands of former colonial subjects from North Africa continued to arrive in metropolitan France. Jews like the Attal family, originally from the Algerian city of Constantine, arrived in France as citizens. Muslims, however, had to apply to the government for the privilege of citizenship.

Benzine also noted 'the unfortunate reality that the Palestinian tragedy fuels the perception among many Muslims that we somehow have the Jews of France to blame'. Another factor, he said, is the so-called *concurrence des mémoires*. 'We have this competition of who's suffering most,' Benzine said. Many French citizens of West African origin, for instance, argue that while the French state has invested fully in preserving the memory of the Holocaust, it has made little effort to preserve the memory of slavery. 'The disparity is a fact, and it's true that many black people say, "Look what they do for Jewish people, and there's nothing for us,'" Louis-Georges Tin, an activist and the former director of the Representative Council of France's Black Associations (CRAN), told me recently. Paris is home to one of the world's premier Holocaust museums and research centres, and a black plaque adorns the façade of nearly every building in the city from which a Jewish child was deported during the Second World War. All that commemorates slavery in Paris, the capital of a former slave-trading nation, are two small nondescript statues. The only museum that documents this history is in the overseas department of Guadeloupe, nearly seven thousand kilometres from mainland France.

But the *concurrence des mémoires* has also become a trope in contemporary French antisemitism, with those such as the Franco-Cameroonian 'comedian' Dieudonné M'Bala M'Bala engaging in Holocaust denial supposedly as a means of attacking 'Jewish power' and insulting what they see as an establishment narrative of the past. Tin said he could understand that frustration but not its expression. 'The anger should not be targeted towards Jewish people,' he said, 'but against the state.'

*

The battle over antisemitism in contemporary France often comes down to a war of words. Few would dispute the existence or even the virulence of antisemitism. According to statistics announced in November 2018 by then prime minister Edouard Philippe on the eightieth anniversary of Kristallnacht, antisemitic incidents in France increased by 69 per cent in the first nine months of 2018. Among those incidents were the torching of two kosher shops in the Paris suburbs and a Jewish teenager being slashed in the face with a

utility knife. For Philippe, the significance of this problem is not up for discussion. 'Every aggression perpetrated against one of our fellow citizens because they are Jewish resounds like a new shattering of glass,' the prime minister wrote. But when it comes to naming the perpetrators or labelling particular acts, this certitude collapses. Much of the French government and the French press can seem at a loss for words.

For many on the political right antisemitism is essentially a straightforward problem, which the left strategically ignores, downplays or denies. 'It's very simple,' Alain Finkielkraut, one of France's most prominent public intellectuals, told me. 'The new antisemitism is an import. It comes to us from the exterior. It's among the gifts, the contributions, of immigration to French society.' (This is not entirely accurate: if the perpetrators in antisemitic crimes are often from immigrant backgrounds, they are almost always also French citizens, a distinction often lost in the public debate.)

Finkielkraut is himself the son of immigrants, Polish Jews who came to France to escape persecution and who eluded the round-ups of the early 1940s. A member of the Académie Française, France's most elite literary circle, he is now something of a public contrarian, a former leftist who uses his bestselling books and radio presence to bemoan what he sees as a nation in inexorable decline. What particularly aggravates Finkielkraut and his conservative allies about the debate around antisemitism in France is what they see as a widespread refusal to 'name the problem' – that is, to declare unambiguously that the primary threat to France's Jews comes from France's Muslims.

For much of the left this amounts to a dangerously crude generalisation about France's largest minority group, which itself is the target of a constant stream

For years the satirical magazine *Charlie Hebdo* had published cartoons of the Prophet Mohammed under the banner of freedom of expression. Its clash with the fundamentalists began in 2006, when the French magazine was one of the very few to republish the cartoons from the Danish newspaper *Jyllands-Posten*, which led to a torrent of protests and threats. On 2 November 2011 it published a special edition focusing on the victory of the Islamist faction in the Tunisian elections entitled 'Charia Hebdo': the editor-in-chief was Mohammed, who adorned the cover beneath the legend '100 lashes if you don't kill yourself laughing'. The same day there was a fire at the offices, with no casualties. On 7 January 2015 *Charlie Hebdo* commented on the publication of Michel Houellebecq's novel *Submission* (which imagines an Islamised France under sharia law) with a cartoon stating, 'Still no attacks in France', to which an armed bearded figure replies, 'Just wait. We have until the end of January to present our best wishes.' A few hours after the news-stands opened, the prophesy came true: the magazine's offices were attacked by the Kouachi brothers, Parisians of Algerian origin linked to al-Qaeda, who had grown up in an orphanage and were radicalised in prison. They killed twelve people, including a policeman during their escape. Two days later Amedy Coulibaly burst into a kosher supermarket, taking seventeen people hostage. Four of them died. In September 2020, to coincide with the opening of the trial of those involved in the 2015 attacks, *Charlie Hebdo* republished the controversial cartoons. A few weeks later an eighteen-year-old Pakistani turned up outside the magazine's former headquarters, wounding two people with a meat cleaver.

of hateful rhetoric, from the covers of *Charlie Hebdo* to the regular pronouncements of sitting members of the French government. Muslims, too, are frequently victims of hate crimes. In June 2018 French authorities thwarted a right-wing plot to kill veiled women, imams and other Muslims at a network of halal groceries, mosques and community centres across France. Authorities charged a group of ten conspirators – one woman and nine men – for terrorist activity; the alleged ringleader was a former police officer.

Cécile Alduy, a scholar who has written extensively on political rhetoric, puts the question this way: 'How can you denounce a "new" form of antisemitism that would be perpetuated only by Muslims without targeting all Muslims as a threat to society?'

Even the phrase 'the new antisemitism' is contested. If the old antisemitism was associated with France's Catholic far right, which has hardly disappeared, the 'new antisemitism' is today used almost exclusively to describe Muslim hatred of Jews. In that sense many on the left believe that 'naming the problem' actually makes it worse, enshrining difference in a society that officially recognises none and repeating the kind of racial stereotypes that only exacerbate social divisions. But others, both on the right and in the Jewish community, ask whether Attal and the other French Jews who have been killed since 2003 are collateral damage in an egalitarian social project that was always doomed to fail. They often decry what they call 'ostrich politics', what they see as the wilful blindness of the left with regard to Islam.

One conservative I spoke to, the Jewish historian Georges Bensoussan, echoed this point. He has been embroiled in a debate about racism and Islamophobia since 2015 when, in the course of a heated debate on a radio show hosted by Finkielkraut a month before the Paris attacks, he said, 'In Arab families in France – and everyone knows it but no one wants to say it – antisemitism is something babies drink in with their mothers' milk.' Under France's stringent hate-speech laws, a number of claimants charged Bensoussan with inciting racial hatred by using reductive blanket statements. He was acquitted in March 2017 – one month before Attal's death – but during the period that French authorities were struggling with how, exactly, to label the killing, the Bensoussan trial was constant point of reference.

For Bensoussan, the trial was 'a symptom of the much larger problem, the hesitation to acknowledge the truth'. He noted that despite the persistence of antisemitism among National Front members and supporters, 'none of the antisemitic murders we've seen [in France in recent years] has been committed by the extreme right. All were perpetrated by Muslims, even as most journalists continue to blame the extreme right.'

Bensoussan is correct that mainstream media outlets refrained from emphasising the Muslim background of Kobili Traoré, but it is hardly the case that they blamed the far right. It is also hard to defend the claim that French Muslims are somehow spared public scrutiny. To take one example, what Muslim women wear outside their homes has been among the most frequently debated questions in France over recent years. Meanwhile, political rhetoric around Islam has become increasingly extreme. Nearly every major candidate for the French presidency in 2017 had an official position on Islam, and Emmanuel Macron is still slated to announce a proposal to 'reform' the practice of Islam in France.

When it comes to antisemitism, members of the French government have emphasised that they find themselves in something of an impossible situation: ensuring the safety of certain citizens while preventing the collective demonisation of others. The state takes the security threat very seriously, dispatching heavily armed reserve officers to guard nearly every major Jewish school, temple and community centre in the country. But, for politicians, finding the right words to describe this situation remains acutely difficult.

'To identify the phenomenon and to understand the different ways it works is not the same thing as identifying potential authors of future attacks. We should pay real attention to the Muslims who feel stigmatised by this,' Frédéric Potier, the head of the French government's interministerial delegation against racism and antisemitism, told me recently. 'You have to pay very close attention to the words you choose and how you say them. But at the same time, we have to say something.'

*

On 16 July 2017 France's new president, Emmanuel Macron, gave a speech at a ceremony to mark the seventy-fifth anniversary of the Vel d'Hiv round-up, speaking at length about France's complicity in Nazi crimes. Standing alongside his invited guest, the Israeli prime minister Benjamin Netanyahu, Macron then turned to the present day, mentioning the name of the woman whose case Jewish groups and public intellectuals had, for months, been citing as the latest example of France's indifference to antisemitism. But the name he used was not Lucie Attal.

'Despite the denials of the murderer, judicial officials must now search for full clarity on the death of Sarah Halimi,' Macron said. Calling her Sarah Halimi was not a novel choice. Ever since the killing first made headlines that had been the name most commonly used to identify the

Above: White stones decorate a Jewish grave. **Right:** A market near Lucie Attal's house in Belleville.

'Sarah Halimi soon became less a real human being and more a metaphor put to use in France's culture wars.'

victim. Yet Sarah Halimi was not necessarily the way she was known to her family or in official documents. Sarah was Lucie Attal's Hebrew name, while the surname Halimi came from her former husband, Yaacov Halimi, a psychologist she had divorced decades earlier.

How the woman known in her lifetime as Lucie Attal became Sarah Halimi after she died is a detail no one can quite explain. But the name only intensified the symbolic resonance of her case. The name Sarah happens to be the label the Nazis uniformly used to identify their female Jewish victims, who were stripped of their individuality along with their lives. Halimi also carried its own grim associations. In 2006 the torture and murder of Ilan Halimi became a national scandal, not only because of the brutality of the crime but also because French authorities at the time had initially refused to acknowledge that his killers had antisemitic motivations.

Thus, by the summer of 2017, Sarah Halimi had come to be seen by many as a new Ilan Halimi, the latest victim not only of Islamist antisemitism but also of government silence and possibly even indifference. 'I think "Sarah Halimi" was the most resonant for the Jewish community, the most Jewish name,' Haïm Korsia, France's chief rabbi, told me. 'For some, the recurrence of the two names was striking.'

Gilles-William Goldnadel, the lawyer for Attal's family and a well-known, hard-line right-wing columnist, disputes that the association between his client and Ilan Halimi was a calculated political move. But he acknowledges that names can be powerful public symbols. 'We can consider that "Sarah Halimi" is the name of the

syndrome for the ideological reticence to recognise reality,' he said when we met in his office earlier this year.

Like Ilan Halimi before her, Sarah Halimi soon became less a real human being and more a metaphor put to use in France's culture wars. In most accounts she was portrayed without nuance or individuality. In April 2018 Sarah Halimi – rather than Lucie Attal – became the centrepiece of a widely publicised book entitled *Le nouvel antisémitisme en France*, a collection of essays by prominent journalists and public intellectuals. 'We have to ask ourselves if her death was only an accident or whether it testifies to the spirit of the times,' says Elisabeth de Fontenay in her preface. Again, the allusion to the earlier Halimi case was clear: 'Such a convergence of silences will have represented a perfect model of public denial.'

*

Of all the events on the Parisian social calendar, none quite compares with the annual dinner of the Representative Council of French Jewish Institutions (CRIF). Not merely a gathering of Jewish leaders or a chance to take a selfie with the ageing Nazi hunters Serge and Beate Klarsfeld, the dinner is a gathering of virtually everyone who matters in French public life, including nearly every sitting government minister. Although the main event is always an address by the French president, the point of the evening is to demonstrate that even the most universalist of republics can recognise that its citizens have their particular attachments.

In keeping with Macron's taste for setting and spectacle, the first CRIF dinner of his presidency, on 7 March 2018, was held beneath the Louvre Pyramid. Once again Macron used the Attal case to show he took the issue of contemporary antisemitism seriously. 'I took a stand by calling for the justice department to make clear the antisemitic dimension of Sarah Halimi's murder,' he said, not without a hint of self-congratulation.

By that point the Paris prosecutor, François Molins, had ultimately decided to consider the killing as antisemitic. In his speech Macron did not go on to discuss the Attal case in any more detail, falling back on abstract platitudes: 'We must never falter, we will never falter, in the denunciation of antisemitism and in the fight against this scourge.'

But two weeks later, on 23 March 2018, Mireille Knoll, eighty-five, another elderly Jewish woman – and a survivor of the Vel d'Hiv round-up – was stabbed eleven times in her apartment and left to burn in a failed arson attempt.

The similarities to the Attal case were immediately striking. Knoll also lived alone in a public-housing project in the 11th arrondissement. Authorities later confirmed that one of her alleged assailants was also a neighbour, also a young man in his late twenties and also a Muslim, this time of North African heritage. Members of Knoll's family later confirmed that she had known the young man, identified as Yacine Mihoub, since he was a boy and that he had been in her apartment drinking port and chatting with Knoll earlier on the day of the murder. Mihoub was a known alcoholic with a history of psychiatric problems, but he had long enjoyed a good relationship with his elderly neighbour. Knoll's daughter-in-law Jovinda told me that in years past, when her mother-in-law was unwell, Mihoub had helped her 'a lot'. 'He was the one who'd helped put her to bed,' she said.

REVENGE OF THE BURKA

The *affaire du foulard* sparked the first French debate over face coverings. The year was 1989, the time of Ayatollah Khomeini's fatwa against Salman Rushdie, and all of a sudden Islamic symbols became hostile symbols, as in the case of the three French girls suspended from school for refusing to remove their veils. The ban became law in 2004 when students were prohibited from wearing any visible sign of religious identity. This was followed in 2011 by another law – the first in Europe – which extended the measure to the whole of French public life, even though in this case there was no reference to Islam but a generic prohibition on covering the face – for 'security reasons'. In 2016 attention was turned to the burkini, the full-body swimsuit for devout Muslim women, which was banned from many beaches on the Mediterranean coast. Three years later controversy broke out around another garment: a tracksuit for female Muslim athletes launched by the Decathlon sports chain. Even though other brands had already offered similar models, the fact that a French company was doing so unleashed yet another round of controversy and accusations – open rather than veiled – of 'betraying France and contributing to the Islamic invasion'. And so the running veil was quickly withdrawn from sale. France takes the idea of the secular state very seriously, but bringing in bans is an approach fraught with contradictions, hypocrisy and even laws that counteract each other: thanks to Covid-19 it is compulsory to cover your face (your nose and mouth at least) as in other countries, but in France it is also prohibited. It's enough to make your head spin.

Below: A shop in Belleville selling kosher and halal products.

THE PASSENGER   James McAuley

The news of Knoll's death broke the next day, via a small item in *Le Parisien* noting that an 85-year-old woman had died in a 'mysterious fire'. The day after that, on Sunday 25 March, two things happened that transformed a small fire in eastern Paris into a national scandal. The first was Paris mayor Anne Hidalgo announcing on Twitter that the victim had been a Holocaust survivor. The second was a Facebook post by Meyer Habib, a confidant of Benjamin Netanyahu's and a right-wing member of the French parliament. Before the authorities had released any information about the identities of the killers, Habib cast Knoll as a victim of 'the barbarism of an Islamist'. He then situated her killing in the context of France's recent struggle with Islamist terrorism. 'It's the same barbarism that killed several Jewish children in Toulouse, slit the throat of a priest in Saint-Étienne-du-Rouvray or a gendarme officer in Trèbes,' Habib wrote. The Trèbes attack, in which four people were killed by a terrorist, including the gendarme Arnaud Beltrame, happened on the same day as Knoll's killing and was still receiving wall-to-wall coverage on all major networks.

Knoll's family, meanwhile, had also retained Gilles-William Goldnadel as their lawyer. He immediately sought to link the two alleged perpetrators. 'The two are Muslims who attacked with barbarity women who haven't done anything,' he told me at the time.

This time the French state's response was different. By midday on 26 March François Molins announced that the Paris prosecutor's office would investigate the death of Mireille Knoll as an act of anti-semitic violence. On 28 March Macron went even further, closing the investigation in the court of public opinion: Knoll, he said, 'was murdered because she was Jewish'.

In the days and weeks that followed the killing there emerged a string of facts that did nothing to undermine the cruel intimacy of Knoll's murder but that did complicate the motive long since ascribed to her alleged murderer – especially the allegation of Islamist antisemitism. For starters, Knoll had two assailants, the second of whom, Alex Carrimbacus, was neither Muslim nor of North African origin. Second, Mihoub had no links to any jihadist organisation. In much of the French press he has been treated as the principal suspect, although both he and Carrimbacus have since accused the other of having committed the actual murder, each claiming to have acted only as the other's accomplice. Both are currently in prison, awaiting the conclusions of an ongoing investigation.

Further complicating matters was the story that emerged about Mihoub's personal history with Knoll. In February 2017 Mihoub was imprisoned for having sexually assaulted the twelve-year-old daughter of Knoll's live-in carer. Mihoub was released from prison in September 2017 on a suspended sentence, and Carrimbacus, whom he had met in jail, later told a panel of investigative judges that Mihoub was out for revenge, a claim authorities have not corroborated. 'He told her, "You will pay. I wasn't at the burial of my sister,"' Carrimbacus reportedly said. But revenge seems an unlikely motive, as Knoll had never filed a complaint against him; it was Knoll's carer, the child's mother, who filed the complaint that ultimately landed Mihoub in prison.

Even if Mihoub did kill Knoll out of some form of revenge under the influence of alcohol, there may still have been an element of antisemitism to the act – what Zagury, the psychiatrist in the Attal case, interpreted as the tragic influence of

> '**More than 250 French luminaries, including one former president, signed an open letter calling for French Muslims to demonstrate their fealty to the Republic.**'

'society's atmosphere and world events'. One of Knoll's sons, Daniel, believes there was, saying that the authorities would not have investigated the case as such if they did not have some evidence along those lines. In his interview with the judges Carrimbacus also reportedly said that Mihoub had antisemitic motivations and had screamed '*Allahu Akbar*' during the attack – an allegation widely reported in the French press as fact, despite the dubious source. Mihoub's lawyer, Fabrice de Korodi, vehemently denies the charge, claiming that Carrimbacus was trying to shift the blame. 'The one motive that we can be sure was not involved was that of antisemitism,' de Korodi told me.

Unlike Lucie Attal, Mireille Knoll became an instant national martyr. On 28 March the CRIF, along with several other Jewish organisations, planned a march in Paris in Knoll's honour, from the Place de la Nation to her apartment in Avenue Philippe Auguste. It was an astounding sight: in a country often accused of indifference to the fate of its minority populations, here were tens of thousands of people marching down the Boulevard Voltaire wearing buttons and brandishing signs that bore the face of a murdered Jew. In the crowd I happened to bump into Finkielkraut, who was moved by the remarkable diversity we saw on the street. 'Many Jews felt abandoned by the national community as a whole,' he told me then. 'But I believe today there will be people of all faiths here. That's very important.'

But a different, less harmonious narrative soon emerged. The month after the killing the cases of Mireille Knoll and the woman now known as Sarah Halimi became the catalysts for a blistering 'manifesto' against 'the new antisemitism'. This was an open letter signed by more than 250 French luminaries, including one former president, calling for French Muslims to demonstrate their fealty to the Republic and arguing that portions of the Qur'an should be 'banished to obscurity', which many took to mean redacted altogether. In a response published in *Le Monde* thirty imams denounced antisemitism but also what they saw as the normalisation of Islamophobia. 'Some have already seen a chance to incriminate an entire religion,' the imams wrote. 'They no longer hesitate to say in public and in the media that it is the Qur'an itself that calls for murder.' (Korsia, France's chief rabbi, later told me that he regretted the phrasing of the original manifesto, which he signed. 'What I would have preferred is that we had made clearer the need for contextualisation and interpretation rather than the total abrogation of this or that verse,' he said, referring to the call to edit portions of the Qur'an.)

Looking back on the affair, Daniel Knoll feels that an opportunity was missed. On a rainy October afternoon he received me for tea at the small apartment he shares with Jovinda, his Catholic, Filipina wife, in a suburb of Paris not far from Orly Airport. I asked him how he felt seeing his mother transformed into a national symbol, a metaphor for the threat of Islamist antisemitism – even if there was little evidence her killer had been an Islamist.

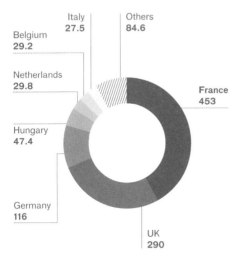

The largest in Europe
(thousands)

Italy **27.5**
Belgium **29.2**
Netherlands **29.8**
Hungary **47.4**
Germany **116**
UK **290**
France **453**
Others **84.6**

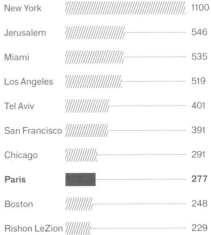

Paris has the eighth largest Jewish population
of any city in the world (thousands)

New York	1100
Jerusalem	546
Miami	535
Los Angeles	519
Tel Aviv	401
San Francisco	391
Chicago	291
Paris	**277**
Boston	248
Rishon LeZion	229

SOURCE: WIKIPEDIA

'The culprit was a Muslim, but he doesn't represent the entire Muslim religion,' Knoll said. He was particularly moved by the diversity of the crowd at the march and what he saw as a collective sense that his mother could be anyone's grandmother. 'But to say she's a symbol? I'm not sure about that.'

Knoll has attempted to take back control of the narrative, publishing a book *C'était maman* in 2018 that explores the values by which his mother lived rather than the circumstances in which she died. It is anything but a testament to the incompatibility of Islam with the French Republic, and he refuses to allow his mother's death to be presented as the failure of *vivre ensemble*, the goal of greater social cohesion in an increasingly diverse society,

which, as he sees it, corresponds to how his mother – the person not the victim – understood the world. The Knoll family, he writes, has Jewish and non-Jewish members from France, the Philippines, Canada and Israel: '"*Vivre ensemble*" could be the title of our family album.'

To honour his mother's memory he is also in the process of founding the Mireille Knoll Association, an organisation that will combat loneliness among the elderly and seek to tackle hatred among young people. The association's vice-president, he told me, is a Moroccan woman and a Muslim. 'Our parents taught us one thing, which can seem naive but which we continue to cherish,' he writes in his book. 'There are no borders for the heart, least of all religion.'

SAPELOGIE(S)

The Societé des Ambianceurs et des Personnes Élégantes (the Society of Ambience-setters and Elegant People), the *Sape*, is a social phenomenon that originated in Brazzaville in the Republic of the Congo. Its practitioners, the *sapeurs*, devoted to the cult of elegance, attempt to outdo one another with their impeccable wardrobes. Accompanied by the *sapeur* Jean-Louis Samba, Frédéric Ciriez sets out to learn about the codes and values that govern this movement of dandies.

**FRÉDÉRIC CIRIEZ
AND JEAN-LOUIS SAMBA**
Translated by Daniel Tunnard

Left: Andy Iris dresses the window of his shop near Simplon.

One day I was walking towards the Marché Dejean, the African market in the Château-Rouge district of northern Paris, when I passed a man dressed in an orange suit, green shirt and matching green crocodile-skin shoes. He walked slowly so the crowd could watch him. Then he started to perform a kind of routine, quickening his step, slowing down, bending suddenly and hitching up his trousers to show off his socks, which also matched his tie ... He was fascinating, eccentric, like a player who comes on stage with the sole intention of baffling his audience. I was immediately put in mind of a sort of contemporary dandy, pushing his search for elegance to the limits, running the risk of ridicule, while also coming across as a genius. He finished his routine, the crowd delighted. I went over and said, 'Sir, I see you are a man of style ... perhaps you work in fashion?' He answered, 'Thank you for thinking me so ... You are dressed like an undertaker from head to toe. But where are you from? You're evidently not Parisian. You've not heard of the *Sape* and *sapeurs!*' I replied, 'The *Sape* and *sapeurs?*' He explained, 'Yes, the S-A-P-E, the Societé des Ambianceurs et des Personnes Élégantes, which advocates the art of being good to oneself, of dressing well and showing off wherever and whenever possible. Those who *sapent* – generally they're Congolese – are *sapeurs*, the classiest gentlemen in the classiest city in the world. Want to know more? Follow me. I'll give you a lesson in style.'

The Societé des Ambianceurs et des Personnes Élégantes translates as the Society of Ambience-setters and Elegant People. *Sape* is also synonymous with the word 'clothes' in popular parlance. The members of the *Sape* are *sapeurs*, more often than not Congolese, who are devoted to a cult of sartorial elegance, living the *Sape* every day like a religion, like a love story. It is a rivalry between Paris and the two Congos, the Republic of the Congo (RC), the former French colony with its capital in Brazzaville, the mother country of the *Sape*, and the Democratic Republic of the Congo (DRC), the former Belgian colony whose capital is the titanic, feverish Kinshasa, where *Kitendi*, the cult of the god of clothing, is practised 24/7. But, above all else, the *Sape* is a journey, at once spatial and aesthetic, an individual quest to the outer limits of a total art, undoubtedly the most beautiful connection between not France – for a *sapeur* there is only Paris – but the City of Light and the two Congos, devastated by colonialism and civil wars.

So how has the *Sape* spread throughout Paris over the decades? An examination of each letter in the word *Sapelogie* might help us to understand. The term *Sapelogie*, the science of the *Sape* – a hybrid concept, at once initiatory and political (and, of course, eccentric) – was coined in the early 2000s by the Parisian *sapeur* Ben Mushaka at a time when the RC was recovering from civil war. His goal was to unify this culture and replace machine guns with the only

FRÉDÉRIC CIRIEZ is a French writer. He is the author of the novel *Mélo* (Gallimard, 2013), a Parisian triptych starring a young Congolese, Parfait de Paris, who is a street sweeper by day and king of the *Sape* by night.

JEAN-LOUIS SAMBA was born in Brazzaville, Republic of the Congo, and is an entrepreneur and digital consultant. He is the creator of madeinsape.com, the first consulting and support site for *Sape* projects aimed at institutions and individuals, and is a long-term collaborator with Jocelyn 'Le Bachelor' Armel, the president of the Republic of the *Sape* in Paris.

In the final decades of the 19th century the European states' interest in a 'place in the sun' in Africa intensified. For centuries white settlers and traders had mainly stayed along the coasts, strategically positioned during the slave trade, but now they began to explore areas of the interior as well, such as the basin of the Congo River where King Leopold II of Belgium decided to found a colony. But around the same time a French naval officer named Pierre Savorgnan di Brazzà also arrived, founding the settlement of Brazzaville in 1881 in the western part of the basin, and the division of the spheres of influence was ratified by the Berlin Conference of 1884–5. (It should be noted that until 1908 the Free State of Congo was not a colony but a private kingdom answering directly to Leopold II.) In 1960 both former colonies gained their independence. The larger of the two, the Democratic Republic of the Congo (which now has a population of almost 100 million and is the world's largest francophone state) with its capital Kinshasa, came under the control of President Mobutu, a dictator who flirted with the USA, renamed the country Zaire and ruled until 1996. The former French colony with its capital in Brazzaville ended up within the orbit of the Soviet Union, and as a result was renamed the People's Republic of the Congo; today it is simply the Republic of the Congo or Congo-Brazzaville and has a population of just five million. The smaller Congo also has its own strongman, General Denis Sassou Nguesso, who, between 1979 and the present day, has only relinquished the reins of power between 1992 and 1997, a situation that has at least ensured greater stability than in the neighbouring DRC, which has suffered decades of civil war.

true weapons that are worth a damn: the clothes and the values of the *Sape*.

S ociety. The S that opens this word is the mystical letter of the *Sape*, the keystone, one that says the *Sape* is an open group, constantly moving, making a break with established social norms. In short, a 'successful' society, rising from the ruins of other societies that were colonised then decolonised. The *Sape* expects nothing from you, but you are always welcome, whether you're black, white, Congolese, a lawyer, a bricklayer, a man, a woman or even a couple. The only rules are that you love yourself, live in the 'I' mode, distinguish yourself with your dress and strut your stuff at every opportunity.

The art of the *Sape* is often associated with clothes alone, but that would be a mistake. In fact, dress is just one –albeit number one – of three main elements, ahead of the art of the parade (*diatance*) and the art of verbal sparring (*nkelo*). Jocelyn Armel, known as Le Bachelor, is a kind of president of the Republic of the *Sape* in Paris, creator of the brand Connivences and director of the famous boutique Sape & Co, located at 12 Rue de Panama in the African quarter of Château-Rouge in the 18th arrondissement. He sums it up nicely: 'Before you open your mouth, you've already been seen.'

To put it another way, *sapeurs* are exhibitionists who exist only for the gaze of others. No audience, no *Sape*. No admiring society, no *sapeur* moving eccentrically in the *zone des pas perdus*, the zone of the lost steps, where you have to take risks to draw attention to yourself, discreetly opening your jacket with its scarlet silk lining. No public, no *nkelo*.

Image, deportment, words: these are the three dimensions of the *Sape*. There is a whole world and knowledge in each of these

Above: On the streets of Château-Rouge.

elements, and the great *sapeur* combines all three on the streets of Paris, a space for staging a performance and, above all, constant risk-taking. With no confrontation – of imagery, of choreography, of words – there is no *Sape*, no quest for a unique style.

Africa. The *Sape* in Paris would not exist without its African source. And the name of that source is Bacongo, a neighbourhood in Brazzaville that is the very symbol of the *Sape*. A pride and an 'ontological' advantage when *sapeurs* are asked where they are from. Papa Wemba, the greatest singer and promoter in the history of the *Sape*, himself originally from the Belgian Congo on the other side of the Congo River, acknowledged this unequivocally. Pure *Sape* comes from Bacongo in Brazzaville and not from the home of the rival *Kitendi* school of Kinshasa.

The *Sape* as practised in Bacongo is formidable. It is a total *Sape*, in which the warriors who commit to do battle with words have innumerable means to humiliate any Parisian *sapeur* who throws down the gauntlet on their glorious return to the country (known as *la descente*, the descent). *Pauvreté oblige*, and with their words they compensate for not being able to afford the clothes they dream of. The Brazzaville *Sape* is highly codified, a game of complex variations around the manner in which you wear a suit or any other item of clothing that shows a perfect 'fine-tuning', a *Sape* that differs widely from the *Sape* of Kinshasa, which is more unbridled, more pop, more globalised and focused on brand worship.

If you encounter a *sapeur* in Paris wearing a Yohji Yamamoto cap with its label dangling like a trophy, that's a *Kitendiste*. If you come across a *sapeur* in Paris showing *himself* off, revealing the luxury brand he's wearing only at the end of his display,

that'll be a member of the Brazzaville school. It goes without saying that the two schools, while in some ways united in their extravagance, exist in a state of perpetual rivalry: the harmony of the 'overall execution' of the outfit versus the bling of the luxury brand ...

Paris. No one can call himself a *sapeur* unless he's been to Paris at least once in his life. Paris is on his mind every day, even if it takes him twenty years to finally get to the city of his dreams. His pilgrimage requires the most detailed preparations: difficult farewells with the family, the drawing-up of a budget, consulting city maps, the must-see places, how to get from different Métro stations to the most prestigious addresses where the creators are to be found ... Those *sapeurs* who have never yet set foot in Paris already know their way around! As soon as they arrive they are welcomed by a delegation of 'Parisians' who take them under their wing and offer them clothes worthy of their new status.

But why Paris? During the colonial period this was the city that imposed images of luxury, of fashion and of the easy life of the white man, whose elegance was to be imitated and even surpassed. After independence it became the city to which generations of *sapeurs* sought to emigrate. Once they'd made it they would be welcomed into the arms of the Maison des Étudiants Congolais (MEC, the House of Congolese Students). Now closed, it was located on Rue Béranger, a stone's throw from the former offices of the *Libération* newspaper and from a legendary place where *sapeurs* could strut their stuff: the Place de la République.

For Djo Balard, the sacred king of the *Sape* in Paris in the 1980s, the *Sape* is a protest movement defined by the rejection

> 'The *sapeur* is absurd, larger than life, too much. He spreads joy, affirmation of the euphoria of the present through the image of the character he has created for himself.'

of poverty and the political institutions of the RC created by Congolese students on returning to their home country after studying in Paris. It is therefore as much a cultural movement as a political one, a claim to a different life. This is part of the answer, but there are others over the countries' long histories, such as the ancestral importance of fabrics and jewellery in the Kingdom of Kongo before Portuguese colonisation and the arrival of Christianity in the late sixteenth century, as mentioned in the remarkable work *Au cœur de la Sape: Mœurs et aventures des Congolais à Paris* by Justin-Daniel Gandoulou, a son of Brazzaville and the first to introduce the *Sape* as a subject at a French university.

Energy. That's what fuels the *Sape*, what gives expression to the *sapeurs* and boosts their eccentricity. Go to the Marché Dejean and witness how the crowd stops because a *sapeur* is putting on a show after a hard day's work on a building site, like a prince descending on the city wearing his smile like any other garment. A child says, 'Oh, he's dressed like a clown!' The kid is right. The *sapeur* is absurd, larger than life, too much. He spreads joy, affirmation of the euphoria of the present through the image of the character he has created for himself. In a Parisian setting, where competition between *sapeurs* is fierce, it's the ultimate pleasure.

This is the grail: not the simple social norms that inform the lives of the *petit bourgeois* but to become one with the admiring crowd on the sacred soil of Paris. This is what's at stake, it is the fullness, the aristocracy of being, the magnificent present rather than the fleetingness tinged with melancholy typical of the ephemeral/ infinite dialectic of the Baudelairean dandy.

Lieux (Places). While Paris as a whole shines in the imagination of the *Sape*, the city can be subdivided into a number of mythical places that feed a cult of neighbourhoods and addresses. Every night in Brazza legends are told about Paris; you hear the songs that carry the names of places you already love, you hum standards by Papa Wemba, like 'Champs-Elysées' and 'Matebu', or even 'Place Vendôme' and 'Victime de la mode' written by Modogo Gian Franco Ferre. The songs recount the real lives of *sapeurs*, where they have shone, loved, had a rendezvous with their mistress. 'My love, I am on the Champs-Elysées … I miss you, I'm waiting for you to come.' Another song explains how to get to Yves Saint Laurent, detailing the route, which Métro line you should take.

Apart from the famous monuments in front of which you can have your photo taken, *sapeurs* also know all about the right brands and boutiques, such as J.M. Weston at 55 Avenue des Champs-Elysées, where the wealthiest (or those with long lines of credit) are greeted like government ministers and order personalised footwear that can take a year to make. It really could not be easier for a novice Congolese *sapeur* to

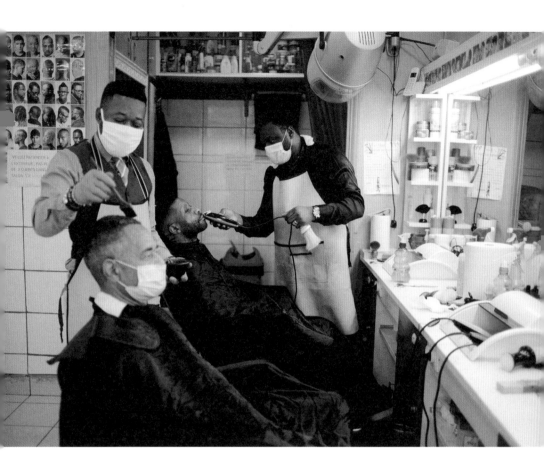

Above: The barbers of Degama-Styl at work.

Above: Andy Iris, owner of the clothing store that bears his name.

THE PASSENGER   Frédéric Ciriez and Jean-Louis Samba

Above: Gaspard Kiakembo is the proprietor of Degama-Styl, where Gaudin Kitumbu (**below**) is one of the barbers.

Above: Serge Kizito from Degama-Styl.

find his way around Paris. His only anxiety is the gaze of the whites, whom he does not know and whom he dreads encountering in the *Sape*'s historic meeting places – Bastille, République, the great boulevards, the Arc de Triomphe, Concorde – and the nearby palaces – the Crillon, the Ritz, the Meurice – and Galeries Lafayette for shopping.

But seriously, you aren't going to dress at cut-price chain Tati and have your photo taken outside an Ibis budget hotel, especially when you live just outside central Paris in the 93, Seine-Saint-Denis, the poorest department in France (see the sidebar on page 52). For a *sapeur*, living in the centre gives one a clear competitive advantage, as the conventional wisdom of the *Sape* says only too clearly: it's better to have a studio apartment in Paris than a mansion in the provinces, for when you live in Paris you live the *Sape* every day, you breathe in the shops daily, you're in the Champions League.

There are two Métro stations that merit your attention: Château-d'Eau and Château-Rouge, both on Ligne 4. Paris's African beauty parlours (hairdressers, cosmetics shops) are around the former, while the food shops and the Marché Dejean are near the latter. The *sapeurs* of Brazzaville or Kinshasa have always had a strong presence in these two districts – perhaps, as one story goes, drawn by the chic air of the word *château*. And then Rue de Panama, in Château-Rouge, is home to J.A. Le Bachelor's boutique Connivences. A stroke of genius. This saint of a man founded and built up this essential establishment, succeeding in bringing the chic of Congo Brazzaville to a working-class district of Paris. The town hall in the 18th arrondissement has done its bit, too, by helping local designers and supporting the young and very hip clothing brand Maison Château Rouge.

Orality: this is the most hidden side of the *Sape*, where the international language is French and the mother tongue Lari, the language of verbal jousts, the *nkelo*. Lari is spoken in Brazzaville and in the south of the RC, while in Kinshasa *sapeurs* speak Lingala, but they have to know some Lari to be able to joust and not be labelled *ngaya*, ignorant. Only the toughest of the *sapeurs* dare undertake the *nkelo* with its extraordinary mix of Lari and French. The best always speak last: sartorial appearance, movement and, finally, verbal attack. While the clothes should speak for themselves, the most skilful will always have the last word and will seek, above all, to show themselves off and destroy their adversary while never – on pain of disqualification – attacking them on the grounds of social identity.

The big *nkelo* in Paris often take place at private parties – birthdays, weddings, funerals and the like. Party organisers will let it be known beforehand that major figures of the *Sape*, which has its own star system, will be in attendance. In fact, any assembly of *sapeurs* is a potential verbal joust, whether in the street or in the café on Rue des Poissonniers. In the event of defeat, the pain and the *humiliation saperétique* are immense and can have consequences on the personal life of the *sapeur*, including separation from their partner or the loss of disciples if they have a school. By contrast, for the victor – never proclaimed as such but palpable in the audience's attitude – glory awaits.

Guerrier (Warrior). *Sapeurs* are 'warriors of appearance': the most Dionysian are in Kinshasa (naked torso under a Cavalli fur coat), the most purist in Congo Brazza (perfectly tailored, pin-sharp suits). Despite their lack of disposable income, they are strong and

Barber
❶ **Degama-Styl**
99 Rue de Clignancourt, 13th arrondissement

Restaurant
❷ **Jennifred Mienandi**
14 Rue de Panama, 18th arrondissement

Bar
❸ **Sape Bar**
12 Boulevard de Denain, 10th arrondissement
❹ **Le Comptoir Général**
80 Quai de Jemmapes, 10th arrondissement

Tailors
❺ **Sape & Co**
12 Rue de Panama, 18th arrondissement
❻ **Andy Iris**
13 Rue Joseph Dijon, 18th arrondissement

Records
❼ **Le Grenier d'Afrique**
3 Rue de Suez, 18th arrondissement

ready to go to Paris to do battle and make a name for themselves. They are co-opted, they have help in getting there; rivals are received, brothers welcomed.

In Paris the longer-settled *sapeurs* find the language of the *Sape* in the verbal creativity of Lari, which has also made the journey from Brazza. For the *nkelo*, a good Parisian *sapeur* must keep himself abreast of what's new in the language of origin. During the jousts it is important to make an impression on others through one's image and voice; to mark them for life, to foster a creative process within them, to be talked about, to become legendary. Every victory is acted out like a great battle.

Among the *Kitendistes* the star *sapeur* is the one who has acquired the most *non-dopés* (genuine) branded clothes and has thus provided for himself through his purchases (the battles) the means to wear the most prestigious collections throughout the year. Among the purists of the Brazza school, the *grand sapeur*, although a great consumer of brands, favours the overall look, the combination of his clothes, which he wears like armour, like finery.

I mmortal. Just as the Académie Française has its *Immortels*, a sort of retirement home for men of letters on the Quai de Conti beside the Seine, so, too, does the *Sape*, the difference being that these have truly made their mark on their art.

Papa Wemba, of course, 'the most complete', music, clothes and politics; dressed by his compatriot Christian Enfant Mystère and coached by Jacques Moulélé, alias Moulé-Moulé, a member of his orchestra Viva la Musica, it was Wemba who validated the *Sape* as a life ideal, breaking with the poverty of the Congo. 'Well dressed, well shaved and well

'Among the purists of the Brazza school, the *grand sapeur*, although a great consumer of brands, favours the overall look, the combination of his clothes, which he wears like armour and finery.'

perfumed.' He is the father of modern *Sape*, the connection between the two Congos and Paris.

Strevos Niarcos, singer, founder and pope of the *Kitendiste* religion, who is commemorated every 10 February in Kinshasa, the day of his death in a Parisian hospital. On that date the paths of the cemetery turn into a catwalk.

Djo Balard, 'king of the *Sape*' since the 1980s, who has reigned between Paris and Brazza, is an exceptional performer and provocateur. He came up with this magnificent sporting proposition: 'Let's organise a *Sape* world cup to show that the white man has no taste.'

The triumvirate of the 2000s is comprised of **Ben Mukasha**, the father of *Sapelogie*, **Rapha Bounzeki**, a *sapeur* musician who has sung the *Sape* in Lari, and **J.A. Le Bachelor**, former collaborator of fashion designer Daniel Hechter and creator of the Connivences brand, which revolutionised *Sape* by introducing colour into the clothes (previously, the *Sape* had not been colourful or flashy). He is now the boss, the initiator of 'affordable *Sape*' for Africans, selling Italian-made suits at €600 ($700) in the ultra-working-class district of Château-Rouge. No appointment is required to go in and talk clothes with the master in his lair on Rue Panama.

As for the younger Immortals, **Gims** was born in 1986 and was formerly a rapper with the group Sexion d'Assaut, composing the 2015 hit 'Sapés comme jamais' ('Dressed Like Never'), which paid homage to the

sapeurs of previous generations – his father, the musician Djuna Djanana, was a fellow traveller of Papa Wemba's. The video accompanying the song is an exceptional portrayal of the fantastical universe of the showbiz version of *Sape*, where all the strands come together. Gims is a *sapeur* by heritage and family culture rather than by any personal claim; nonetheless, in paying homage to the movement, he brought it out of Papa Wemba's 'Sape ghetto' and into the spotlight as something Parisian, French, international, transcultural and transgenerational.

The list of Immortals also includes the stylists who make the clothes and accessories that the *sapeurs*, with whom they are often friends, wear: Marithé + François Girbaud, a cult label in 1980s Paris, the iconoclastic Jean-Paul Gaultier and not forgetting Japanese designers like Yohji Yamamoto and Takeo Kikuchi, whom the *Kitendiste sapeurs* are mad about. Tokyo is itself a *Sape* stronghold, a city where creators have always respected *sapeurs*, often inviting them to fashion shows, something that French brands rarely do.

*É*cole (School). I, Jean-Louis Samba, co-author of this article with Frédéric Ciriez, want to tell you about my own *descente* in Brazzaville in 2015 after twenty years in Paris so that you will understand the high personal stakes involved in a *sapeur*'s return to the home country, crowned in the glory of being a P, a Parisian. That particular moment when

> 'The days when people might say that the *Sape* was just a way to entertain white people have long gone. It is now emancipated and aimed at Africa, proud of its heritage and of its young Paris-based creators.'

a Congolese P goes back to his roots, validating his odyssey to the capital of the *Sape*, is essentially a moment of recognition. Papa Wemba celebrates it in a song set to a Congolese rumba called 'Proclamation'. Paris is a constant test; the return to Kinshasa or Brazzaville is the validation of that test before declaring victory.

I am from Ouenzé, a neighbourhood in north Brazzaville. Although I consider myself to be an occasional *sapeur*, the pressure is on all *sapeurs*, whether part- or full-time, to 'make the return', the first since their departure for Paris, and in doing so demonstrate one's symbolic success. I thus had to distinguish myself, do something striking for my *descente* so that my compatriots would feel deep down that I had undeniably become a P, polished, elegantly styled and with an impeccable wardrobe. I had noticed that no one making their *descente* in recent times had gone for a daily change of outfit. I kept my plan secret and prepared for a three-week stay: twenty-one days meant twenty-one pairs of shoes, twenty-one pairs of socks, twenty-one shirts, twenty-one suits, twenty-one pairs of chinos plus plenty of gifts for my nearest and dearest.

As my flight was delayed for three hours, I didn't arrive in Brazzaville until after dark, thus disrupting my plans to make a splash as I left the airport. Having failed on that score, I hopped into my brother's taxi to go and greet my mother in Ouenzé. He left me a kilometre away from the house so I could be seen in my capacity as a P, but, walking at night through a city with no street lighting, I was invisible. Another failure.

I was happy to see my mother again, and she blessed my arrival. Then I left and took up my rooms at the Acacias, an inn situated a stone's throw from the very working-class Marché Total in Bacongo, a neighbourhood in the south of the town where things happen.

An uncle called me early the next morning. 'Jean-Louis, you must do better, this isn't working.' Message received and understood. I put on a new outfit and went out in broad daylight. People were already waiting for 'the Parisian' outside. I showed myself off, and boy did the public validate my return!

Every day that followed I triumphed in a previously unseen outfit. Concerned, J.A. Le Bachelor and J.C. Nkoyi of the Andy Iris label, whose schools I represent, each called me one day after the other. 'Do you want me to fly you over a suitcase of clothes? Are the *sapeurs* giving you a hard time?' They needn't have worried. Success and recognition were mine. My family was proud of me. I had avoided disgrace and earned their admiration. I made it from Paris to Bacongo.

(S) stage. Paris is the stage of the *Sape*, and so it will remain. The days when people might say that the *Sape* was just a way to entertain white people have long gone. It is now emancipated and aimed at Africa, proud of its heritage, and its young creators,

It was in the early 2000s that an eccentric Ivorian by the name of Douk Saga visited the Atlantis, a nightclub popular among black Parisians, and decided to challenge a group of equally flashy young men to see who had the most money. His stunt of burning banknotes caught the public's attention, and he quickly gathered together a group of like-minded individuals who called themselves the Jet Set and created their own style based on extravagance, ostentation and the flaunting of wealth but also *joie de vivre*, a carefree attitude and a new style of dance music. The result was coupé-décalé, which, in Ivorian Nouchi slang, means take the money and run. 'Sagacité', Douk Saga's first hit, encapsulates all of this: high-end boutiques, cigars, grand hotels and dancing in front of the Eiffel Tower. With its frivolous lyrics, danceable rhythms and with entertainment as its sole objective, the new genre was also a way of holding your head high and sending out a signal of hope to your countrymen back home living through the First Ivorian Civil War. So before long the echo of coupé-décalé from the clubs of Paris reached Ivory Coast, becoming a regional musical phenomenon that spread to the whole of francophone Africa. The biggest star of the second generation, who took the genre into the mainstream, was the Ivorian DJ Arafat who later died in a motorcycle accident. Following a tribute concert held at the national football stadium in Abidjan in August 2019, which was attended by thousands of people, many fans, struggling to come to terms with the death of their idol, made their way to the cemetery in which his body had been laid to rest. Some managed to break through the security cordon and opened the coffin to inspect the corpse, checking the tattoos to confirm that the person buried there really was the king of coupé-décalé.

like Goya and Natty Kongo Création, are based in Paris. Likewise, young French labels such as Vicomte A, as well as well-established brands like Paul Smith and Louboutin, are keen to add a touch of the *Sape* to their own collections.

The *Sape* is part of today's sensibility, speaking to young black men in the working-class suburbs and attracting the attention of whites. Naturally, all its stars are in Paris: Victime de la Sape and his style based on vintage clothing; Stany de Paris, the master of the movement; Norbat de Paris, popular and with a strong media presence; and, of course, the *Kitendiste* brothers from the DRC, like Trésor Ngando ('the Crocodile'), nicknamed 'King Yohji Yamamoto', and Robby Gianfranco. The next generation is ready.

The *Sape's* vitality does credit to Paris, a city of sights with two million people (and a metropolitan area of more than twelve million, the Grand Paris that politicians like to spin). The profound beauty of this art, the historic scars that it covers beneath the stitching of beautiful clothes, its post-dandyism, its sacrificial power that is so economical that you have to spend and consume a lot (Georges Bataille and Jacques Lacan are never far away) make it an intoxicating continent open to all. An open society. An inalienable part of Africa in Paris. 🐟

Paris Syndrome

The French capital is notorious for its unforgiving treatment of outsiders, whether they are tourists or inhabitants of the 'provinces' that comprise the world outside the capital and Île-de-France. These are the chronicles of a provincial-turned-Parisian.

BLANDINE RINKEL
Translated by Daniel Tunnard

Left: Crows rooting for food in a litter bin in Les Halles.

'Paris is thus filled with provincials, who spend their careers there and flee as soon as they can. Marseilles, Lyons and Bordeaux no doubt have genuinely indigenous populations, which date back several generations and possess their own peculiar characters, traditions, culinary specialties, and slang. But Paris is like a huge pump, which alternately sucks up and spews out provincials.'

— Michel Tournier, *The Wind Spirit*

1

It was a friend who told me first. We'd just witnessed a violent crowd incident in the Métro. An elderly woman had got herself trampled on the platform for not getting on to the train quickly enough. People pushed and shoved at the automatic doors, shouting over each other, and the woman, motionless in the midst of it all, fell. Poor thing.

Half shocked and half blasé about this all-too-common scene, I whispered to my friend that it must be tough for tourists to discover that Paris is like that; I imagine they don't expect it to be that way. Probably not, no, Anne replied, and, like any good Parisian who can't help digging up a quotation, she added, you know, there's a psychiatric syndrome related to the disappointment that foreigners can feel on arriving in the city. It's called Paris Syndrome. Not everyone in the world of psychiatry is convinced it exists, she added, but it's interesting on a – shall we say – literary level. It factors in a number of symptoms faced by some visitors to France, particularly tourists from Japan. They suffer delirious states, hallucinations, feelings of persecution, but they might also experience palpitations, sweating ... And, on seeing the surprised look in my eyes, she laughed that little laugh, which from a distance sounded like it contained a hint of pride, and concluded that discovering Paris must indeed be testing.

I found that fascinating.

That night I looked into the matter. From what I could find from googling, the problem in question affects around fifty people each year and is caused by the huge gulf between the idealised image that the Japanese have of Paris and the actual city that they find. Reality, as Lacan said, is when you bump into it.

The Japanese in question go to pieces because they never imagined there would be shadows in the City of Light. Because an attack in Pigalle is unthinkable to them. Because they expect all the women to look like Audrey Tautou and the men like Alain Delon. Because back home no one chucks cigarette butts into the street or crashes into you on the escalator.

And because, more than anything else, they did not expect that hardly anyone in Paris would have the time to help them

BLANDINE RINKEL is a French writer, musician and journalist who works for the magazines *Gonzaï*, *Citizen K* and *La Matricule des anges* as well as at the radio station France Inter. Her literary debut, *L'abandon des prétentions* (Fayard, 2017), was shortlisted for the Goncourt Prize for a debut novel; her latest, *Le nom secret des choses* (Fayard, 2019), was the starting point for this article.

understand the street signs and decipher the French. 'If you don't speak the language people act like you don't exist,' one tourist said in an article on this subject in *L'Express*. I found that easy to believe.

Or, rather, I found it troubling to believe. It saddened me a little when I thought about it again, mulled it over. And from mulling it over I realised that if I had felt touched by this syndrome as soon as I heard about it, it was because I, too, in my own way, had experienced it.

2

I had just arrived in Paris. I was eighteen years old and had just left my family and my childhood behind. It was a new world to me. Like the 322,000 other students who go to university here – one in ten Parisians is a student – I had 'gone to the capital' to study because I believed my childhood reading in Rezé, my small home town in western France, would have been ample preparation to allow me to thrive there.

I had no idea my town would be referred to as 'provincial'. I had never before heard the word, which is used to describe everywhere in France that isn't Paris, and, although I don't remember where I heard it first, I do remember that it made me laugh as I found it so imprecise. One could not very well include the likes of Lyons, the Jura and the small town of Plougasnou in Brittany under a single blanket term. It just didn't make any sense. And yet, in Paris, it did.

Culture was a very precise thing here. It wasn't French culture in its entirety, it was a particular culture, a culture that the sociologist Bourdieu, as I would learn, had renamed *legitimate culture* and which was called in the most important schools' competitive examinations *general culture* or *general knowledge*.

I didn't expect to be intimidated by this culture.

I didn't expect to have to hide my personal tastes.

I didn't expect to be ashamed to have once sincerely loved musicals, the film *Amélie* or the *Star Academy* musical-talent show.

I didn't expect the violence of Paris.

Or that this city would alienate me.

I didn't expect, ultimately, to alienate myself.

Between the ages of eighteen and twenty-two, as I discovered Paris, I lived the life of an impostor. I learned the expressions *Marxist thought, hit the news-stands, cinéma d'auteur*. I learned not to love but to know about exhibitions, to give the impression that I hate the Métro, to moan. At university, imitation quickly became my principal hobby.

I faked an understanding of texts read out loud or references tossed into the air in the everyday exchanges that followed classes. I faked by day then caught up by night, consulting Wikipedia until some ungodly hour. Maurice Béjart, Simone Weil, Paul Nizan, I trawled the internet for all those names I had never heard of, stockpiling information.

My cultural lag was an ogre that could never be sated, one of those bottomless bags that become emptier the more you fill them. And the more effort I made to digest this new data, the more I measured the extent to which my general knowledge was and remained provincial – that is, middling, middle class.

I did not have, and never will have, the comfort of my origins.

I lacked the confidence that must come, I imagine, from having shelf after shelf stuffed with books in one's Haussmannian apartment, books that one must have read, books whose titles count three times as much at dinners with cultivated old France, that serve as passwords granting

Above: Travelling on an elevated section of the Paris Métro.

THE PASSENGER   Blandine Rinkel

Above: A student at a Parisian school takes a break.

their subversive children entry into the right sections of society, the liberal anarchists, the bourgeois Marxists. Anne had such bookcases, and I envied her for that. I lacked the self-confidence that you must derive from having spent your first nights out on the same streets that appear on the Paris Monopoly board, having studied at the top schools in *L'Express* magazine's rankings, where one can indifferently opt for courses in Chinese or film, your first wanderings under the statues of Danton, Henry IV or beneath the Eiffel Tower – a monument about which Parisians couldn't care less, as I later discovered.

I learned that it was bad taste to love the Eiffel Tower and marvel at it, and ceased to marvel. More generally, I ceased to be too emotional, to laugh too loud, to cry. I learned to mask my character traits, to cease to be astonished by everything that happened. People are never surprised here. I controlled my face. Little by little this mask of serenity would become another one of my traits. I learned to mask. To this day I still feel a sense of betrayal for those years of discreet imitation.

I wasn't familiar with the names people dropped but sought nonetheless to know them, and that was what I had to hide, always denying. I had to feign insouciance when in reality I was quite overzealous. It was also the case that I was afraid, as physical and mechanical as that. I was afraid of not having read what I ought to have read, afraid of being one of the masses, a little clumsy, a little too spontaneous, afraid even of the sound of my own laugh, which was too pronounced, as if my whole body relaxed when I laughed. And so I misrepresented myself. I held myself. I caught up and shut up. Sometimes at night, in secret, I still read some of the bestsellers that my new crowd looked down upon, but I did this in the way that one asks after an old friend and, finding less and less pleasure in doing so, I stopped bothering in the end.

I soon learned that in Paris people didn't lunch at twelve nor did they dine at seven, that everything begins an hour or two later. Even the timetables were different. And so at nine I had dinner, listening, exuding confidence, my interlocutors nodding at the most aberrant comments with a smile, eternally calm, eternally *au courant*, as if I already knew in advance what I was yet to learn, playing at being a snob. But snobbery wasn't a game to me, it wasn't a joke; it was a form of violence.

The violence wasn't physical, it was symbolic.

All those who are called provincials, a fortiori from the middle classes or the poor, have no doubt experienced this cultural violence. It seems to be a French particularity, as it is more intense here than anywhere else.

Of course, the likes of Martin Eden or Billy Elliot exist everywhere, but nowhere is the concentration of power and culture as strong in the capital city as it is in France. And nowhere is culture, generally speaking, so essential as it is in France. Across the world Paris is seen as the global capital of luxury, fashion, haute couture. It is no accident that UNESCO, created after the Second World War to promote education, science and culture, has its headquarters in Paris. There is such a concentration of museums, of concert halls, of unheard-of cultural events, all of which explains, while not justifying, the assumed arrogance of its inhabitants.

It took me almost ten years to put into words what it was that bothered me about these people we call Parisians, but there it was: self-importance.

The inhabitants of the capital – and I now count myself as one of them – come across as self-important, and it is this,

'It took me almost ten years to put into words what it was that bothered me about these people we call Parisians, but there it was: self-importance.'

I believe, that makes them so irritating. What I mean by self-importance is that Parisians seem to be self-sufficient. They have no need to go anywhere to satisfy an urge for culture, for food, for a social life. They rarely travel, and the Parisian woman, in the stereotype we have of her and which Inès de La Fressange or Catherine Deneuve embody perfectly, gets about by bike wearing a floral dress and heels with no fear that she will come to any harm, for she will not venture far (see 'The Parisienne' on page 85). As we imagine them, Parisians have everything at their fingertips and little curiosity about regions other than their own, which, as I have said, they refer to collectively as the provinces.

Faced with all that, we tend to be ashamed of our own inadequacies.

I was ashamed.

Authors like Annie Ernaux (*Shame, The Years*), Didier Eribon (*Returning to Reims*) and Édouard Louis (*The End of Eddy*) have explored this embarrassment of coming 'from elsewhere' and the decision you can make on arriving in Paris to draw a line under your origins and reinvent yourself completely by changing your name or by cutting ties with your family.

In *Returning to Reims*, an examination into society and family, Didier Eribon portrays the good student from a working-class background who, having gone to Paris, is forced into a 'near-complete re-education' of himself in order to enter another world, fascinated by the discovery of literature and Marxism, and who soon comes to resent his parents for, on the one hand, being uncultivated while, on the other, not embodying the proletarian ideal.

There is a paradoxical violence when you replace the home town of your childhood with a Parisian setting, naturally intellectual, a violence that forces you to discover that you don't really know how to fight for your own rights, that *you lack the words* to describe your own situation. I recalled the Japanese woman's words in *L'Express*, giving them new meaning: 'If you don't speak the language people act like you don't exist.'

For the preceding ten years I had been living in a game of *Trivial Pursuit*, which had made me feel ashamed without being able to explain why.

A game in which I had been anxious about not being able to speak the right language, about not existing.

A game in which I had been afraid of being unmasked as a provincial.

Being unable to explain: every time I had attempted to put into words the abyss between my idea of culture on arriving in Paris and that of Parisian intellectuals, I came up short and felt inadequate. I felt like an idiot. My all-too-rational words seemed incapable of transcribing the mystique that presided over my embarrassment. The sensation that I had when I was younger that people in the world of culture – writers, for example – were a different species, semi-divine, unattainable, radically *separate*.

For a long time I thought – and the thought does still come to me – that I was cut off from the laboratory where culture is made by a *magical* barrier.

I must insist on the word magical. In my mind at the time it wasn't a social barrier or a geographical one, nor was it a professional or economic hurdle – it

Above: Lost in thought at a party.
Left: A sticker saying *rêve générale* (general dream), a play on the words *grève générale* (general strike) (**top**); rush hour on the Paris Métro (**bottom**).

Paris Syndrome

Île-de-France represents:

■ with regard to France   ● with regard to Europe

Île-de-France

AREA

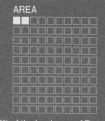

2% of the land area of France

POPULATION

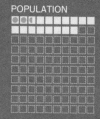

18% of the pop. of France
2.4% of the pop. of Europe

WORKPLACES

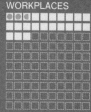

23% of all jobs in France
2.8% of all jobs in Europe

GDP

31% of French GDP
4.6% of European GDP

RESEARCH FUNDING

40% of R&D funding in France
6.5% of R&D funding in Europe

SOURCE: INSEE AND EUROSTAT

CONTRIBUTION TO NATIONAL GDP

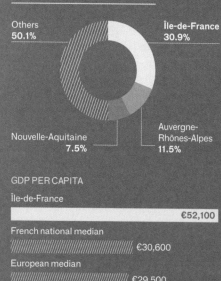

Others
50.1%

**Île-de-France
30.9%**

Nouvelle-Aquitaine
7.5%

Auvergne-
Rhônes-Alpes
11.5%

GDP PER CAPITA

Île-de-France

€52,100

French national median

€30,600

European median

€29,500

SOURCE: EUROSTAT (2019)

ÎLE-DE-FRANCE VS. THE PROVINCES

Price differences between Paris
and the provinces

Communications	+0%
Alcohol and tobacco	+0.5%
Clothing and footwear	+2.9%
Furniture, household appliances and routine maintenance	+4.2%
Transport	+5.7%
Food and non-alcoholic drinks	+6.4%
Health costs	+6.5%
Free time and culture	+6.6%
Restaurants and hotels	+8.0%
Other goods and services	+9.9%
Rent, maintenance and accommodation	+24.7%

SOURCE: INSEE

was a *magical* barrier. And this feeling of magic, this *a-cultural* feeling, was hard to share with my new friends. It couldn't be dissected into various kinds of social determinism; there was an ineffable feeling that I just couldn't talk about.

If they understood my situation, it was always through a Bourdieusian prism – rational, political – and so it was that out of respect, without meaning any harm, they would quote Godard and the Pinçon-Charlots, left-wing references approved of and desirable in this new environment, and I failed to make them understand this one crucial thing, that their constant references to Bourdieu seemed to me to be the first of what he himself calls 'symbolic violences'. The exact words, the *so-right* words that they had at their disposal to speak about class struggle, which my parents didn't even know existed, only *reproduced* the violence.

I had palpitations; they had references.

3

But times change, and in recent years shame has morphed into hatred.

Physical violence answers symbolic violence.

For better or for worse, France is wreaking its revenge on Paris.

Many books from the 2010s attest to a growing anger at the privileges of the capital. *Désintégration* ('Disintegration') by Emmanuelle Richard, to give one example, is a novel steeped in hatred for 'this little group [in Paris] who take pleasure in everything and despise the working classes'. It is a political novel that analyses how a certain contempt from the upper classes breeds anger. What triggers it in this case? One afternoon the narrator hears some young people on a Parisian street repeating the phrase 'What can I do? I don't know what to do', which Anna Karina chants

in Jean-Luc Godard's *Pierrot le fou*. It is shameless, writes Emmanuelle Richard, who goes through several jobs but still can't make ends meet. And so, 'faced with the novices who shout about their privileged idleness, she thinks of her parents, modest state employees who have watched powerless all their lives as their aspirations have narrowed', and she discovers an urge to violence.

An urge not to explain any longer but to put an end to the self-importance of the socially privileged.

In 2019 the anger of the *gilets jaunes* expressed that same desire.

On the first weekends of the demonstrations the rallies brought around ten thousand people together in Paris to protest against rising petrol prices and the cost of living. Soon Fouquet's, the famous brasserie on the Champs-Élysées, had been vandalised, the Palais Brongniart in the Place de la Bourse had been attacked, the railings of the Tuileries had been uprooted (causing a serious injury) and news-stands had been set alight. In response, the forces of law and order hit back with a vengeance. According to the Ministry of the Interior, 1,900 *gilets jaunes* were injured, ninety-four of them seriously – a cut hand or facial injury – and fourteen people lost an eye. But everywhere in the beautiful neighbourhoods the desire remained the same: to put an end to the privileges of the rich, even if it meant losing a limb. 'Bring France up to Paris' and set it on fire. On social media, a call went out to 'fetch Emmanuel Macron'. (See 'The Avenue of Revolt' on page 27.)

In March 2020, during the first Covid-19 lockdown, the anger at Parisians departing for the countryside to avoid being crammed in with three other people in the forty square metres of space that the average Parisian occupies certainly reached its apogee, and articles by some

Above: A view of Paris through the dirty windows of the Pompidou Centre.

'Those friends I met when I arrived in Paris, such as Anne, were they not also mostly renters themselves? Did they not have money troubles, too? They were cultured, true, but did they really live in luxury?'

THE PASSENGER   Blandine Rinkel

bourgeois writers – who claimed, like Marie Darrieussecq in *Le Point*, that they had to 'hide their car with its Paris registration plates in the garage' so as not to be attacked – only fanned the flames of further mocking and more urges to kill someone on Twitter.

But is this fair?

Are all Parisians really as privileged as we imagine?

According to a 2019 study by the letting agency LocService, rental prices in Paris are on average 188 per cent higher than in the provinces, and almost two-thirds (61.7 per cent) of inhabitants in the capital rent their main residence compared with only 40 per cent nationwide. Paris is also one of the three most polluted cities in France (along with Lyons and Marseilles), and Parisians on average spend one hour and thirty-two minutes in transit every day. Cultural attractions and career opportunities are, of course, flourishing, but there is no longer the same quality of life, so Parisians are leaving their own territory en masse. According to the French National Institute for Statistics and Economic Studies (INSEE), the capital currently loses around twelve thousand inhabitants annually (although a similar number arrive each year). Between 2011 and 2016, 59,648 people left the capital and seven in ten inhabitants of Île-de-France claim they still want to leave the capital and its region. That they don't all take the plunge is mostly for fear of unemployment. Because the situation for the working classes in Paris – financially, socially and in terms of general welfare – is becoming increasingly precarious. After fifty years of gentrification the percentage of blue-collar workers in the city has dropped from 65.5 per cent to 28.6. Every multi-millionaire wants a pied-à-terre in the capital, but Paris has more than ten thousand homeless. In 2015 the poverty rate reached 16.1 per cent. Meanwhile, the middle classes do what they can in the city and, although they know they're making a pact with the devil, willingly sublet their apartment on Airbnb to help make ends meet, something they would struggle to do otherwise.

Furthermore, those friends I met when I arrived in Paris, such as Anne – whom I also believed at first to be a snob – were they not also mostly renters themselves? Did they not have money troubles, too? They were cultured, true, but did they really live in luxury? Wasn't their situation more ambiguous than first impressions might have suggested?

Back at my mother's, seeing the quality of life she now enjoys, a retiree in her small town, I think again about the so-called snobbery of the Parisians and among my friends as well, and it appears to me suddenly to be the clear expression of some kind of malady, a defence of some sort. It was all they had. References to mask their own discomfort.

Paris Syndrome. When it comes down to it, Anne and many Parisians were perhaps the first to experience it. Perhaps that was why it fascinated them, they knew how contradictory Paris is, how attractive, how violent.

They must also have experienced a lack of clean air or of nature and the freedom that comes with it. They, too, must also have had the sense of being wounded.

Living in Paris, I told myself, you relate to the culture, to certain codes, to a certain irony or a game, because you can easily guess the rest.

You feel and you know everything that you're missing. ✒

This article is an adapted extract from *Le nom secret des choses* by Blandine Rinkel (Fayard, 2019).

A Season
with Red Star

BERNARD CHAMBAZ
Translated by Daniel Tunnard

Red Star players warming up before a match at the Stade Bauer, Saint-Ouen.

In the heart of Seine-Saint-Denis, the notorious department 93 is home to one of France's oldest football teams, one that has links to the wartime Resistance and a philosophy of anti-racism and anti-fascism: welcome to Red Star FC.

In football, the year 2014–15 was one and the same, what we call a season, which runs from autumn through winter to spring. That year I was lucky enough to spend time with the Parisian club Red Star FC. I followed the team, come rain or shine, and I loved every minute of it, cheering the players on as they battled their way to promotion into Ligue 2, the French equivalent of the English Championship, which used to be called the Second Division. Then the team went back down again, but it's ready to come back up and was a whisker away from doing so in 2020 when Covid-19 brought everything to a halt.

What defines a football club is its history, and Red Star's is as long as it is illustrious. A club is also its home ground, and the Stade Bauer is nothing less than a monument. A club is also a specific urban space, in the case of Red Star a town – Saint-Ouen-sur-Seine – on the northern outskirts of Paris, in Seine-Saint-Denis, the poorest and most deprived department in France. And, of course, it is also its players, and during my season following the team I enjoyed getting to know them both on and off the pitch, and I will introduce you to some of them a bit later.

Although it is not the oldest football club in France – that honour goes to Le Havre Athletic Club, established by British expats – the history of Red Star does date back to the 19th century. Jules Rimet – the man who created the World Cup, no less – was the club's founder. If we think of him now we might imagine an old gentleman in an overcoat, three-piece suit and top hat, just as he appears in photographs, but what we should remember is that on that fateful day, 21 February 1897, he was just twenty-three when, with his brother Modeste – that really was his name – and two friends, he founded this club with an English name. The famous *étoile rouge* had nothing to do with any Bolshevik future, rather Red Star was a shipping line, British, just like Miss Jenny, the Rimet brothers' governess.

It is perhaps not known as widely as it might be that Red Star won five Coupes de France. The first three were consecutive wins, in 1921–3, at Paris's Stade Pershing in front of thirty thousand spectators; the fourth was in 1928 and the fifth during the Occupation, on 17 May 1942, in the stadium at Colombes to the north-west of Paris, in heavy weather for the time of year and with heavy hearts all round. I love the words of Fred Aston, the winger who scored the winning goal. 'We had played in the tournament all year, and we made it to the end. We had to be happy – that's only natural – but it would have been better at any other time.' The champagne must have tasted bitter; that same month the Vichy government brought in the STO (Service de Travail Obligatoire), the forced-labour programme that sent young men to Germany and which led Rino della Negra to go into hiding to avoid enlistment. He was the first Red Star player I ever heard of.

Saturday 21 February 2015 was the seventy-first anniversary of Rino della Negra's execution at the hands of the Nazis. He had worn the number-seven shirt before he joined up with the FTP

BERNARD CHAMBAZ is a French novelist, essayist, poet and author of biographical and sporting books. His writing has earned him numerous awards, including the Goncourt Prize for a debut novel in 1993 for *L'arbre de vies* (F. Bourin), the 2005 Apollinaire Prize for *Été* (Flammarion) and the Académie Française Roland-de-Jouvenel Prize and the Grand Prix de Littérature Sportive 2014 for *Dernières nouvelles du martin-pêcheur* (Flammarion).

'What defines a football club is its history, and Red Star's is as long as it is illustrious.'

(Francs-Tireurs et Partisans, an armed wing of the Resistance formed by the French Communist Party) and became one of the MOI (Main-d'Œuvre Immigrée, 'immigrant labour') group who gave their lives for France and became the subject of the well-known *Affiche rouge* poster put out by the Nazis following their arrest. He died at the age of twenty, and his last words, sent to his brother just before he went before the firing squad, are etched on my heart: 'Send a hello and farewell to everyone at Red Star!' A memorial was organised outside Stade Bauer. I went along out of a sense of moral imperative and gratitude. At 2 p.m., in front of the plaque, there weren't a lot of people, just big grey clouds. The first to arrive sheltered in the café opposite, then more appeared, about thirty in all, some young, some old – some even older than me – members of the Friends of the Resistance and of the National Veterans Association, their flags draped over the palm tree in the square and later run up the flagpole during the delivery of a short speech under an ever-darkening sky. Then we laid flowers, five bouquets, and I was angry with myself for not bringing a red or a yellow rose. Finally, there was a salute to the dead, with no bells or fanfare, but as the first raindrops fell those present struck up a timid 'Marseillaise' and then a more rousing 'Le chant des partisans', which was cut short, drowned out by the engine of the 166 bus.

A stadium is central to a club's identity, and this is especially so in the case of Red Star. We often read in the press that 'Stade Bauer was electric', and it's no exaggeration to say that this legendary place pulses with energy. It is an English-style stadium – or rather, half a stadium if not a quarter, since two stands have been condemned and the fourth was never built because the housing secretary didn't get on with the sports secretary. A low-income housing block stands behind the goal on the town hall side. From their balconies the block's tenants can either watch the match or gaze over towards the Sacré-Cœur, whichever takes their fancy. The stadium has been there since 1909, inaugurated with a match against an English team with the wonderfully old-fashioned name of Old Westminster. The stadium is a beacon of social diversity, something that sports journalist Jean Eskenazi wrote about: 'This was never a place for snobs. This was not Paris. It was better than that. It was Paname.' That said, Paname, an old nickname for Paris, has disappeared, but Red Star's stadium will never be a place for snobs.

What is the Bauer? A stadium, yes, and a street, too – the stadium is on Rue du Dr Bauer – but *who* was Bauer? Jean-Claude Bauer was a Saint-Ouen doctor who joined the Resistance, was arrested by French police, handed over to the Gestapo and shot. To honour him, the town gave his name to the former Rue de la Chapelle.

If you are heading to the stadium from central Paris, leave the Métro at Porte de Clignancourt, cross Boulevard des Maréchaux, continue due north past a car park then under the Boulevard Périphérique; no need for a compass as you pass the flea market – or, more

PARIS SAINT-GERMAIN

The football team Paris Saint-Germain (PSG) was founded only as recently 1970, and the motivation was political: the last time a team from the capital had won the Coupe de France was in 1949, and a reboot was required. The new team at first merged with Stade Saint-Germain, but a split occurred after less than two years, the plan being to promote Paris FC and relegate PSG to amateur football. Things turned out differently, however, and PSG was saved by the fashion designer Daniel Hechter and other fans, including the actor Jean-Paul Belmondo. Hechter was also responsible for designing the iconic Eiffel Tower logo and the red stripe on the team's shirt. And so began the strange coexistence of a glamour team based at a stadium in a wealthy neighbourhood with a working-class fan base, some of them from the outlying district of Saint-Germain-en-Laye, attracted by the club's affordable pricing policy. The ultras movement also took hold, and PSG's fans became some of the most feared and right wing of any in Europe. In the 1990s the new Canal+ ownership pushed for the creation of a second, moderate, apolitical grouping at the other end of the stadium, leading to open clashes between the two camps. The team also failed to impress in terms of results, but then came the revolution of the past decade: after the death of a fan in 2010 five ultras groups were disbanded and thirteen thousand fans were barred in a joint effort between the club and the police that proved highly controversial after it emerged that illegal profiling had taken place. In 2011 the club ended up in Qatari hands; that France had played a decisive role in the 2010 decision to award the 2022 World Cup to Qatar remains controversial in some quarters. Following this change of ownership, ticket prices rose by 70 per cent, and PSG became one of the giants of European football with money no object, as can be seen from the signing of Neymar for €222 million ($260 million) and Mbappé for €180 million ($211 million).

accurately, the shops and stalls that sell clothes, tracksuits, genuine and fake leather goods, trainers, €50 crocodile-skin shoes, watches, etc. To your left you pass Rue Voltaire, named after the man who wrote *Candide*, as did Leonardo Sciascia, then Rue Biron, honouring a peasant from Cantal who got rich in cattle, and then you hit Rue du Dr Bauer. Before the match people line up at the ticket booths, drink at l'Olympic (the bar across the road), while others queue at the van where the mothers of the young players sell portions of golden fries for a euro. You go up a few steps, and it's always the same sense of wonder. A green rectangle bordered by white lines.

I've dreamed about it, I really have.

After many generations of players, after Lev Yashin, I, too, got my chance to set foot on the turf at Stade Bauer with the French writers' team. I did so as one would in the sacred enclosure of an Olympic stadium or in 'the marble dust' so dear to Lamartine. I had already played on every surface you can imagine: grass, mud (with or without clods, depending on the season), *stabilisé* grass pitches (some better drained than others), not to disregard the concrete of the schoolyard and the cobblestones of Paris and other cities across the world. But here, for the first time, I put my moulded studs on an artificial – that is, synthetic – turf. It was pouring with rain that day, and rain has always made me happy. But I realised immediately that something was missing – the puddles, the slap-slap of the boots, the mud that had made us rejoice when we were children. Instead, the rain actually made the ball move faster, which, from my perspective at least, wasn't necessarily a good thing.

A football club belongs to its space – large or small, urban or rural – and here it is a town, an interface, an ecosystem, a corner of the red neighbourhood, a department.

First, it is the municipality of Saint-Ouen, where the club earned its spurs in the working-class world. These workers came here after being pushed out from a Paris emptied of its inhabitants by property speculation, from the countryside, from foreign countries such as Italy and Poland, from overseas departments and territories, from French colonies when African countries had not yet achieved their independence. In the 21st century the great streams of immigration have stabilised, and the town benefits from this diversity. More than ever the club still has a vocation to attract and draw in local young talent, from the basin, from the *territoires*, from the plain, from the cantons, from everywhere. To give them a chance.

Football allows young people to dream, and that can only be a good thing. In football they see a chance to allow their passion, their gift, to flourish as well as being a pathway to the social success engendered by football's insane financial bubble. French international Kylian Mbappé is from Bondy, fifteen kilometres from Saint-Ouen, part of the same urban fabric.

The history of Saint-Ouen did not begin yesterday; it dates back to the Middle Palaeolithic, which is quite some way back. Ouen was a saint who played for good King Dagobert's team, back when Stade Bauer was just wasteland. At the time of the French Revolution the town was named Bain-sur-Seine, and it wasn't until the July Revolution of 1830 that the port and the docks were constructed. This marked the beginning of industrialisation, which gave rise to the famous red belt, the industrial suburbs of Paris that lie beyond the city walls.

What is certain is that Red Star is the jewel in the town's crown. Some prefer the flea market, the antiques and second-hand market, but not me. The celebrated writer Raymond Queneau did his bit to make the town famous:

The blue or white flower
Has such a hold over my heart.
Has such a hold over my heart
In Saint-Ouen near Paris.

As well as the football club and the flea market the town is home to a large household-waste company and a number of office blocks in which the likes of Danone and L'Oréal have set up their headquarters. For decades the number of inhabitants has been stable at around fifty thousand, of whom around thirty thousand earn a wage. The unemployment rate pre-Covid-19 was around 18 per cent, almost twice the national average but lower than the municipalities in the less central areas of the department. Two-thirds of the population is under forty-five. In other words, Saint-Ouen presents the classic face of a municipality in the inner suburbs (the *petite couronne*, the first ring of departments around central Paris). In this context you can see the club's legitimate desire to appear and define itself as *populaire*, working class. But what is a working-class club?

In this context you can see the club's legitimate desire to appear and define itself as working class. But what makes a club *populaire*?

First of all, it is its distinctiveness. What sets Red Star apart from other Parisian clubs – it is not Paris Saint-Germain with all the glitz and glamour of big-money football, nor is it on the same shaky ground as Paris FC – is its long and brilliant history; second, it is its ideal location on the edge of what was once called 'the zone', the crossover territory between the capital and the suburbs, for the last fifty years the entity of Seine-Saint-Denis; so,

putting together its history and its location, what makes it unique are its roots. But what does it mean to be *populaire*? In football, the cheaper sections of the terraces are *populaires*, often standing only, behind the goals, where the noisiest element of the crowd urges on their team – although there are no terraces behind the goals at Stade Bauer. We can understand the adjective *populaire* both for its positives (genius, wisdom, folk dance) and its negatives (gullibility, prejudice), and the list of synonyms ranges from 'vulgar' to 'famous'. That said, the definition of the word is unambiguous: 'that which belongs to the people, which characterises the people', not only those who come to the stadium for a price you might think reasonable but also those who play there. So you can see the players as a reflection of the crowd and the young people as a breeding ground.

To use a buzzword, you could say that Red Star is an *institution*. Since 2008 it has had an outstanding president in Patrice Haddad, founder of the Première Heure advertising production company, passionate like most presidents but discreet, humanist, a lover of art and literature who wears a Kangol cap. At his side are Pauline Gamerre, a general manager with a great future whom I have had the pleasure of meeting on a number of occasions, David Bellion, an unusual creative director and footballer of rare elegance who is also passionate about the arts, and Steve Marlet, the director of sport, who shone here as a player at the end of the last century. At the age of five he was already swift and skilful. He had a remarkable football coach, an old guy with a gammy leg, whom he respected. He did well at school, putting in enough work to be left to his own devices, and he preferred playing football to watching it on TV. When he was twelve he was spotted by the sports-and-studies section of Saint-Germain-en-Laye,

Above: L'Olympic, the bar where Red Star fans meet before home games;
the bar's toilets (**below**) are decorated with the team's stickers and political messages.

A Season with Red Star

THE PASSENGER   Bernard Chambaz

but the boarding school was expensive, and a fracture to his fifth metatarsal meant he had to leave. He then made a beeline for Seine-Saint-Denis, the 93. He grabbed the phone book and called every club. Bobigny welcomed him. That was where he was recruited by Red Star and quickly made his way into the first team. Eventually he moved to Saint-Ouen, 7 Rue Blanqui, sharing a flat with a view of the stadium from the dining-room window. What followed was beautiful: a rich career, big clubs, three major leagues (France, England, Germany), caps with the French national team, titles.

While a coach isn't, strictly speaking, part of the 'institution' as such, Christophe Robert was none the less the artisan and the architect of the 2015 promotion to Ligue 2, and he shares the honours with his staff. In his office opposite the gym disorder reigns – desks piled high with computers, index cards, copies of the *Le Parisien*, a set of scales, a washbasin – and on his wall an Eric Cantona quote that is what it is and is less cryptic than his famous statement about seagulls and sardines: 'I don't play against a particular team. I play against the idea of losing.' Robert's role model is Arsène Wenger. He came back to the 93 after passing through Ivry and Espérance Sportive de Zarzis in Tunisia, which left him with many a fond memory, the stadium in the desert, the matches in front of twenty or thirty thousand spectators, a 'crazy atmosphere'.

Although they don't make the club, the players do make the team that is, for a time, the soul of the club. Think of Platini at Juve, Maradona at Napoli, Steven Gerrard

If Paris were a separate country it could win the World Cup. A team made up of the gifted players born within the city's metropolitan area, led by Kylian Mbappé and Paul Pogba, could hold their own against Brazil or England. At the 2018 tournament, fifty-two of the players were born on French soil, including many who play for other nations, from Morocco to Senegal. No fewer than fifteen were Parisian, enough for a full team plus substitutes. In the past twenty years the city has produced more top-class footballers than any other in the world: between 2002 and 2018 sixty Parisians played in the World Cup. Although these numbers reflect the capital's multiculturalism, thanks to which many footballers with dual nationality can play for other countries, the phenomenon is growing ever more pronounced and relates above all else to life in the Parisian *banlieues*, where football is seen as a way out of poverty. Local authorities also play their part: almost every municipality has a football team partly financed from municipal funds. The creation of the Clairefontaine National Academy, where footballers like Thierry Henry, Nicolas Anelka and Mbappé learned their trade, dates back to 1988. The decision to locate the national stadium, the Stade de France, in Saint-Denis for the 1998 World Cup was also designed to regenerate the area, like the structures being built for the 2024 Olympics. While the wait for economic and social progress in their neighbourhoods stretches on indefinitely, young *banlieusards* dream of becoming the champions of the future, like their predecessors who look down at them from huge (sponsored) murals. The one dedicated to Mbappé reads: '*Bondy, ville des possibles*', 'Bondy, the city of possibilities'.

Dating from 1909, Red Star's Stade Bauer is one of the oldest in France. Its current appearance, with the iconic triangular apartment block replacing one of the two ends, dates back to a 1975 renovation. In 1999 the ground's state of disrepair was aggravated by a storm that triggered almost two decades of debate between proponents of renovation, supporters of a transfer to a new home and those who want to see a new stadium rebuilt on the same site. It is no longer suitable for first- or second-tier fixtures, so when Red Star were promoted to Ligue 2 in 2015 they were forced to emigrate to Beauvais, seventy-five kilometres from Paris. Such is the bond between the Bauer and Red Star fans, though, that some hoped for relegation in order to bring the club back 'home'. They were soon obliged by the Saint-Ouen outfit's disappointing results, but the club took steps to be ready for a renovation if and when they return to the second division. Things seemed to be falling into place during the 2019–20 season, and, although an agreement was signed for a new ground that would be part of the works for the 2024 Olympics in parallel to the restoration, the dream in the shorter term was to go back up to the second division and to adapt the stadium for the more prestigious stage. But the arrival of Covid-19 put paid to the plans; the championship was suspended, Red Star stayed where they were and the dream of renovation faded, with only the new-stadium option still being examined. Just the simple matter of who will build it remains: in a surprise move, the municipality of Saint-Ouen refused to sell the land to the company (Réalités) that won the tender in order to hold discussions with one of the unsuccessful bidders. Presumably they're used to siding with the underdog.

at Liverpool. Taking a closer look at the team that I got to know during the 2014–15 season, we'll begin with the goalkeepers.

Vincent Planté wore the number-sixteen shirt and the captain's armband. He had a happy childhood, taking part in gymnastics, roller hockey and football. But why play in goal? When he was six he turned up for his first training session. Two goalkeepers were needed, so the coaches chose the two tallest players. At his first youth team he had a good coach who taught him the essentials and how to hold the ball with his Mapa gloves. Following a spell at a training centre he embarked on a career that eventually brought him to Red Star. He was one of a small group of players with impressive longevity. He set himself a cut-off age of thirty-five, which he stuck to and retired in 2016. 'My body let me know,' he said. He wanted to pass on to his three children what his parents had taught him. To accompany them with his wife to training and to matches, to the nursery, to school, so they could mix with other people. Honesty and upright behaviour were most important to him. When I asked him which colour football shirt he preferred to wear, I was disappointed by his response. It was all the same to him! What he cared about was the result.

Born in 1991, Bobby Allain wore the number one, even though he was the reserve goalkeeper. At the time he was one of the oldest at Red Star (having previously played on the turf at Stade Clerville in Ivry-sur-Seine, another illustrious red-belt municipality just south of Paris). He owes his surname Allain to his father and his first name Bobby to his mother, who was a big fan of J.R.'s little brother in the series *Dallas*, which finally wound up the year he was born. Another thing he owes to his mother are his Scottish roots. Between the ages of sixteen and seventeen he played for

Above: Red Star fans cheering on their team from the stands,
while (**below**) the players work hard on the pitch.

A Season with Red Star

'One great thing about this superb old club, is the attention it pays to its youth and cultural development programmes.'

Clyde in Cumbernauld just outside Glasgow. His fondest memories of both football and holidays (when he can tell the two apart) are linked to Scotland; he was amazed at the atmosphere on match days as well as during training, the players' commitment, the fans' passion, and he found some of that same spark at Red Star. When he had some free time he didn't really explore Scotland much, not venturing any further north than Loch Ness, because he spent most of his time playing football with his cousins. He said that his favourite colour shirt was green; however, during the 2014–15 season the goalkeepers alternated between yellow and red. His role model had always been Gianluigi Buffon, that towering figure of goalkeeping who wrote an astonishing autobiography, *Numero 1*, which Bobby said he hadn't yet read.

Red Star has, in fact, been home to a number of prestigious goalkeepers over the years. The first, Pierre Chayriguès, stood only 1.7 metres tall on the tips of his toes. His career started before the Great War, and he came from the local club Clichy. He was born on either 1 May or the day after – whichever way, just in time for the all-new Workers' Day. He was the first to come off his line, to punch balls away, to dive at strikers' feet or just dive – horizontally. He said it himself clearly enough, because he later wrote a book: 'I understood straight away that the goalkeeper had to be something more than a man locked in his goal.' He continued after the Great War, easily identified by the unique way he tied his bootlaces – twice around his ankles – that was copied by the kids who idolised him. After the Second World War he retired to the seaside and opened a café. Another goalkeeper was Julien Darui, one of the first foreign-born players to find glory in French football. He made his debut for Olympique Charleville with his friend Helenio Herrera – who went with him to Red Star and was the inventor of the tactical system in football known as *catenaccio* – along with Arthur Rimbaud, the poet with 'soles of wind'. Darui was the flying man. As well as his prowess in diving for the ball, he excelled in clearances, with his feet as well as with his hands. To make ends meet and put some money in the bank, he ended up at Cirque Pinder. Cheered on by an audience delighted to see this bonus act between the clowns, the big cats and the bass drum, he made a living by saving penalties for the crowd's entertainment. He did this for a season then opened a bar out in the countryside.

But it's not just about goalkeepers; a football team needs outfield players, too.

During the 2014–15 season Samuel Allegro was our number fourteen, like Cruyff. He was the first player anyone mentioned to me when I arrived at the stadium, the vice-captain, the star, and all the kids wanted a number-fourteen shirt. Brave, unassuming, with an exemplary mentality, he had remarkable footballing qualities combined with an uncommon intelligence that led him to state that the mistake that he found easiest to forgive was a refereeing error.

Ludovic Fardin had at the time been at Red Star for fifteen years. Given that he was twenty-nine then, it doesn't take a maths genius to work out that he'd spent half his life there. He's local, from Seine-Saint-Denis, and proud of it. Born in Aubervilliers, he grew up in La Courneuve, went to a Jules-Vallès school, got into football at seven or eight, enrolled at CMA, the Municipal Club of Aubervilliers, a people-oriented place. There he was scouted by a Red Star coach, and he joined the sports-and-studies department at the Michelet College close to the stadium. He played and he studied – 'My parents wanted me to work hard at school.' He took the ES (economics and social sciences) baccalaureate, the toughest to pass. For a challenge he tried out at Matra Racing in Colombes, in department 92, but it wasn't to his liking. Despite its proximity to the 93, Colombes feels further away than you might think, the atmosphere not so warm, as if the 92 were another world. So he worked at McDonald's and then as a postman in Bondy. The main post office was at the end of the Rue de la Philosophie. I'm not making this up; think about it. Ludovic continued to play for amateur teams while delivering the mail and came back to Red Star when the Aubervilliers coach moved there. Promotion came after five years. 'I'm staying here, the club's put its trust in me,' he told me. The 93 was his home; he was living in Bobigny, between Aubervilliers and Bondy.

One great thing about this superb old club is the attention it pays to its youth and cultural development programmes. The management sets out to instil manners in its young players – and in the corridors of the club's buildings and on the pitch I never came across a kid who didn't greet me with a clear 'Bonjour'. With a sensitive, intelligent approach to football they will become good players – and the future of any club is surely its young players – but they won't necessarily end up playing here, as the best will be snapped up by the big European clubs and the less passionate or the less fortunate will end up who knows where.

During my season at Red Star I had the pleasure of spending time during the All Saints' Day holiday in their company, and we had a go at writing our own little footballing dictionary. Here are my favourite entries: **ball** – our dream since we were kids; **control** – technical skill that is the basis of football; **pass** – a Cantona quote, 'the best goal I ever scored was a pass' (I had to explain to them what Cantona meant by this, however); **foot** – seat of intelligence; **nil-nil** – not necessarily nothing.

And finally, a club is also its supporters. Red Star fans have a history as long as their club's, and it would be remiss of me not to give them a mention. They have unique songs, both funny and salutary: 'Cop, soldier or referee, what wouldn't you do for money?' I met a long-standing supporter, Thierry Chaboud (who passed away in May 2020); he joked that he was a man of letters because he worked at the post office; he was a trade unionist, well liked by his colleagues at the post office as well as fellow fans on the terraces. He loved rock music. He had been going to Stade Bauer since the 1970s and never missed a game if he could help it. He was a little kid from Saint-Ouen who had worn out the seat of his shorts at the Émile Zola School and the soles of his shoes on the asphalt of Avenue Gabriel Péri. With his old-fashioned modesty and good nature he embodied the club. And, as much for his attitude as for his memories, he passed on his passion to the young.

And there we encapsulate, in just a few words, the magic of Red Star. ✈

The Fifteen-Minute City

TERESA BELLEMO
Translated by Alan Thawley

Robert Doisneau's image of a couple kissing by the Hôtel de Ville was chosen by *Life* magazine to illustrate Parisian life. Beyond the almost obligatory focus on the city's established reputation for romanticism in the eyes of the world, the activity surrounding the embracing couple is a pretty faithful portrayal of another of the city's defining features: the bustle, the pedestrians, the mixture of authentic Parisians rushing to reach a specific destination with walkers – or, rather, *flâneurs* – moving more slowly with no schedule to stick to, tourists intent on snapping the riverside on their phones while ensuring a clear enough view of a section of the Eiffel Tower, just a glimpse, a little to the left.

More than just a journey from point A to point B, walking in Paris is almost a way of being. It is one indisputable benefit of the city's approach to planning, which provides pedestrians – at least in the central arrondissements – with broad pavements, an ever-increasing number of traffic-free routes and mazes of alleys and parks that enable savvy pedestrians to cut journey times while enjoying the carefully tended greenery. This cultural mindset and cityscape are reinforced by the policies of the current mayor, Anne Hidalgo: quite apart from the complex battle over banning traffic along the embankments of the Seine, the gradual extension of the thirty km/h speed limit and the pedestrianisation of nine major squares, her objective is to ensure that all streets in the city centre are bike-friendly in time for the 2024 Olympics and to remove 74 per cent of on-street parking spaces – and within the next twenty years to ensure that every service in the city can be reached in no more than fifteen minutes on foot or by bike. This can only be achieved by a radical change of approach plus a series of funding allocations to build new cycle routes (in addition to the existing thousand-kilometre network) and incentives for businesses to encourage their staff to cycle to work. For a city of more than two million inhabitants this might seem to be utopian thinking, but Paris has always shown itself ready to embrace such challenges. In 2007 it was one of the first in Europe to inaugurate a bike-sharing system – Vélib' – which was an instant success and today accounts for 37 per cent of bike journeys, although other services are also very popular, including scooters.

In contrast to other major cities, a Métro season ticket is not such a necessity in Paris. Why shut yourself up in the belly of the city if you can enjoy what is on its surface? Why not walk from Pigalle to the Louvre or choose a longer route from Montparnasse to take in the

Champ-de-Mars? Of course, it takes a bit more time. And this is perhaps what differentiates Paris from other equally beautiful and languid European cities. Here walking or strolling is an intrinsic part of the city's history, a phenomenon celebrated by Charles Baudelaire and Walter Benjamin and which Benjamin attempted to codify. The definition of a *flâneur* is someone who walks with no particular destination in mind, looking around, analysing and observing what they come across, deriving their desire for curiosity and amazement from the very act of setting out for a walk and leaving behind the indifferent, disenchanted gaze out of a window at a courtyard. There is no sense of the almost alien freneticism of certain cities where thousands (or millions) of people combine to form almost a single entity that walks down the street in one direction or the other – depending on the place and the time of day – or hurries across the road in unison in Shibuya.

Novels set in Paris almost always depict the possibility of leisurely meandering. The myriad adventures of Georges Simenon's Jules Maigret are no exception, as the inspector is another member of that class of idle *flâneurs*. In spite of the taxis and a wife who drives him out of the city (like any real *flâneur* he does not have a driving licence), his strolls along the Quai des Orfèvres, popping into a bistro for a beer, and his slow walks set the tempo for the novels, marking out the rhythm and helping to communicate his state of mind and the stage he has reached in his investigations. The place names are accurately recorded, almost as if intended as a guide for readers, because anyone who loves Paris, even those who only visit for a few days a year, cannot help but read the street names as they explore the city on foot with their eyes open, amazed at what they find.

A Sign of the Times

KAOUTAR HARCHI
Translated by Daniel Tunnard

In July 2020 the French online magazine *Streetpress* published an investigation in which a police sergeant, Amar Benmohamed, exposed serious acts of abuse in the cells of the High Court of Paris, the largest court in Europe. From evidence found in a number of reports, messages and internal documents it appears that over a two-year period more than two thousand defendants, mostly highly vulnerable foreigners, were subjected to physical, sexual and psychological violence.

This casts a dark shadow over the city. How can we square the fact that in France's capital the values of liberty, equality and fraternity exist side by side with acts of humiliation and torture? Some have sought to answer this by claiming that these are isolated, exceptional cases. However, from a sociological perspective, racial violence – understood as a set of assaults on the moral and bodily health of an individual through othering and the demeaning of their supposed or actual origins – however incredible it may be, is never extraordinary but, on the contrary, is part and parcel of the social structures that allow it to take place.

In other words, with regard to such acts taking place at the heart of the Parisian establishment, and questions about the police more generally, we have to consider contemporary law and order in the historical and political continuum of colonialism. Indeed, the way in which the 'enemy within' is constructed has its roots in the counter-insurrectional strategies put into effect by the police and army in the colonies and has been redeployed by the authorities in Paris in their efforts at managing post-colonial migrant populations. Furthermore, it is essential to consider police practices through unequal and discriminatory dimensions. So, in France, nearly all the people who have died at the hands of the police were young, working-class Arab, black or Roma men. According to a 2009 report by CESDIP, the sociological research centre on law and penal institutions, black people are 3.3 to 11.5 times more likely to be stopped and searched than whites; Arabs are generally seven times more likely to be stopped; overall they are between 1.8 and 14.9 times more likely than whites to be stopped by the police or customs at the sites selected. The old colonial security order and the contemporary profiling of specific populations inform the race question in France.

However, while Paris has witnessed numerous race crimes, it is also where the Comité Adama Traoré network emerged, an organisation named for the 24-year-old black man who died on the floor of a police station in Persan, near Paris, in 2016, after being arrested by three police officers. The increasingly powerful minority protests help to progressively construct the race question – as highlighted by the methods used by the police to maintain order – as a democratic challenge. In 2020 Didier Fassin put it this way in *L'Obs* magazine: 'The deaths at the hands of the forces of law and order are merely the tragic, extreme manifestation of this discrimination, and this daily bullying reminds those who are victims that the principles of the Republic don't apply to them and that, contrary to the promises of democracy, their citizenship remains second class. They want to make their voices heard today.'

You can be sure that the coming years will see new ways to address the challenge of achieving genuine equality for everyone.

The Playlist

BLANDINE RINKEL
Translated by Daniel Tunnard

Listen to this playlist at:
open.spotify.com/user/iperborea

Paris is a mixture, and the ingredients come from all over – from Brussels, from the Vendée or from the north – and are exported everywhere – to the south, to Japan, even to the USA and the UK. So it is with Christine and the Queens, an artist from Paris who is so ambitiously up to date that she went global and ended up leaving the French capital to haunt all the major cities of the world. While rap dominates in the 21st century, in recent years it has taken on so many different forms that no one really knows any longer just what it's all about. On the one hand, you'll find PNL, in a video at the top of the Eiffel Tower, whose idea of romanticism is notching up more than 175 million views on YouTube while talking about hash and a basement full of cockroaches; on the other, with no basement and no cockroaches, younger rappers – part of a generation that isn't afraid to show vulnerability and add a little humour – are revitalising the genre and even have the nerve to include choruses with melodies (Lomepal). Elsewhere, young singers revive the ghosts of old-school *chanson* – in the style of Véronique Sanson or Édith Piaf – with a fresh-yet-solemn touch (Juliette Armanet and Clara Ysé), while other artists who defy simple definitions, such as Flavien Berger and Philippe Katerine, change the tune completely and, by means of 808s and Auto-Tune, come up with a more demure version of the form. Paris is a cocktail. You work on your own, with a tendency towards melancholic refrains or ritornelli (Sébastien Tellier), and you work light – a laptop is preferable to lugging heavy instruments around. Bands have become rarer, but solo artists come in every shape and every colour, from the militant variety of Yseult to the elegant and direct pop of Arnaud Fleurent-Didier via the solar electro of Myd or the less-classifiable material of the likes of Muddy Monk, Ichon or Bonnie Banane, examples of quirky, colourful artists producing smooth, well-produced sounds, all of whom show what appeals in Paris today: the bizarre and the cool, the intersection of styles.

1
Flavien
Berger
Pamplemousse
2018

2
Myd
*Together
We Stand*
2020

3
Clara Ysé
*Le Monde s'est
dédoublé*
2019

4
Sébastien
Tellier
La Ritournelle
2004

5
Juliette
Armanet
*Manque
d'amour*
2017

6
Arnaud
Fleurent-
Didier
France culture
2010

7
Philippe
Katerine
Aimez-moi
2019

8
Lomepal
Mômes
2018

9
Yseult
Corps
2019

10
PNL
Au DD
2019

11
Christine and
the Queens
*People,
I've Been Sad*
2020

12
Myth Syzer
(ft. Bonnie Banane,
Ichon & Muddy Monk)
Le Code
2018

Digging Deeper

FICTION

Christophe Boltanski
The Safe House: A Novel
University of Chicago Press, 2017

Virginie Despentes
Vernon Subutex Trilogy
Farrar, Straus and Giroux, 2019–21
(USA) / MacLehose, 2018–20 (UK)

Annie Ernaux
The Years
Seven Stories Press, 2017 (USA) /
Fitzcarraldo Editions, 2018 (UK)

Sebastian Faulks
Paris Echo
Picador, 2019 (USA) / Vintage, 2019 (UK)

Tristan Garcia
Hate: A Romance
Farrar, Straus and Giroux, 2010 (USA)
/ Faber and Faber, 2012 (UK)

Faïza Guène
Kiffe Kiffe Tomorrow (USA) /
Just Like Tomorrow (UK)
Mariner Books, 2006 (USA) /
Chatto and Windus, 2006 (UK)

Mahir Guven
Older Brother
Europa Editions, 2019

Michel Houellebecq
Submission
Picador, 2016 (USA) / Vintage, 2016 (UK)

Sanaë Lemoine
The Margot Affair
Hogarth, 2020 (USA) / Sceptre, 2020 (UK)

Daniel Pennac
The Scapegoat
Penguin, 2014

Wendell Steavenson
Paris Metro
W.W. Norton and Co., 2018

NON-FICTION AND MEMOIR

Sarah Bakewell
At the Existentialist Café: Freedom,
Being and Apricot Cocktails
Vintage, 2017

Jane Birkin
Munkey Diaries 1957–1982
Weidenfeld and Nicolson, 2020

Joan DeJean
How Paris Became Paris:
The Invention of the Modern City
Bloomsbury, 2014

David Harvey
Rebel Cities: From the Right to the
City to the Urban Revolution
Verso, 2019

Philippe Lançon
Disturbance: Surviving Charlie Hebdo
Europa Editions, 2019

Jeremy Mercer
Time Was Soft There: A Paris
Sojourn at Shakespeare & Co.
St Martin's Press, 2005

Elaine Sciolino
The Seine: The River That Made Paris
W.W. Norton and Co., 2019

Luc Sante
The Other Paris: An Illustrated Journey
Through a City's Poor and Bohemian Past
Faber and Faber, 2017

Lindsay Tramuta
The New Parisienne: The Women
and Ideas Shaping Paris
Abrams, 2020

Enrique Vila-Matas
Never Any End to Paris
New Directions, 2011 (USA) / Vintage, 2015 (UK)

Edmund White
The Flâneur: A Stroll Through
the Paradoxes of Paris
Bloomsbury, 2015

Olivier Ayache-Vidal
Great Minds (Les grands esprits)
2017

Bertrand Bonello
Nocturama
2016

Robin Campillo
120 BPM (120 battements par minute)
2017

Mia Hansen-Løve
Eden
2014

Nadav Lapid
Synonyms (Synonymes)
2019

Ladj Ly
Les Misérables
2019

Olivier Marchal
36 (36 Quai des Orfèvres)
2004

FILM

Various directors
Paris, je t'aime
2006

Julien Abraham
Made in China
2019

Olivier Assayas
Non-Fiction (Doubles vies)
2018

Graphic design and art direction: Tomo Tomo and Pietro Buffa
Photography: Cha Gonzalez
Photographic content curated by Prospekt Photographers
Illustrations: Francesca Arena
Infographics and cartography: Pietro Buffa
Managing editor (English-language edition): Simon Smith

Thanks to: Alice Amico, Charles Buchan, Marco Cacioppo, Laëtitia Chhiv, Frédéric Ciriez, Lorenzo Flabbi, Frédéric Gai, Andy Iris, Yasmina Jraissati, Mark Kessler, Gaspard Kiakembo, Simon Kuper, Fabio Muzi Falconi, Arianna Malacrida, Tommaso Melilli, Germán Morales, Lorenza Pieri, Cinzia Poli, Lorenzo Ribaldi, Blandine Rinkel, Olivier Rubinstein, Claire Sabatié-Garat, Alexandre Sanchez, Sara Scarafoni, Paul Souviron, Olivia Snaije, Daniel Tran, Maÿlis Vauterin, Rui Wang, Samar Yazbek

The opinions expressed in this publication are those of the authors and do not purport to reflect the views and opinions of the publishers.

http://europaeditions.com/thepassenger
http://europaeditions.co.uk/thepassenger
#ThePassengerMag

Translators: Arabic – Nashwa Gowanlock (The Fear of Letting Go); French – Jennifer Higgins (The Parisienne), Simon Pare (The Avenue of Revolt), Daniel Tunnard (The Beaubourg Effects, Sapelogie(s), Paris Syndrome, A Season with Red Star, A Sign of the Times, The Playlist); Italian – Lucy Rand (Defying the Stars, sidebars), Alan Thawley (The Fifteen-Minute City, sidebars, editorial, photographer's biography, standfirsts, picture captions)
All translations © Iperborea S.r.l., Milan, and Europa Editions, 2021

ISBN 9781787703223

Printed on Munken Pure thanks to the support of Arctic Paper
Printed by ELCOGRAF S.p.A., Verona, Italy